CRYSTAL
PUZZLE

GROWING UP WITH A SISTER WITH ASPERGER'S

CRYSTAL

PUZZLE

Ashley Nance

Published by Familius LLC, www.familius.com

Familius books are available at special discounts for bulk purchases for sales promotions, family, or corporate use. Special editions, including personalized covers, excerpts of existing books, or books with corporate logos, can be created in large quantities for special needs. For more information, contact Premium Sales at 559-876-2170 or email specialmarkets@familius.com

Library of Congress Catalog-in-Publication Data

2014941302

pISBN 978-1-938301-57-5

eISBN 978-1-939629-51-7

Printed in the United States of America

Edited by Jasmine Ye

Cover Design by David Miles

Book Design by Brooke Jorden

10 9 8 7 6 5 4 3 2 1

First Edition

CONTENTS

∽ 1 ∽

Calm and Confusing

Without conscious thought, I enter the username and password of my e-mail account into the fields as required. The page loads, and there is a message from my parents reminding us to pray for Crystal and to call her at least once a week. I had received an almost identical e-mail a month or so ago, when her last relationship reached crisis level. I wonder what has happened this time, but even before I open the message, I know there won't be any details in the e-mail.

> We are fasting about Crystal's short-term and long-term future this Sunday and would like you to join us. Her time at Scenic View may be drawing to a close. She has demonstrated that she has had a difficult time making good choices about relationships, and it seems to us that her self-esteem needs a boost. We need to decide with Crystal when she needs to leave Scenic View. Either way, she needs a plan for the next twelve months.

As I suspected, I'll have to call and get the specifics from Mom, and Crystal, later.

My name is Ashley. I'm brown-haired and brown-eyed with glasses and freckles—as normal and quaint as can be—but I am not your everyday Ashley. Not every Ashley has visited nine different countries, sung soprano in an all-region choir, ran with her mother as she worked to lose 140 pounds, helped teach teens and adults with severe physical challenges, or learned to speak Mandarin Chinese in Taiwan. And not every Ashley has a sister with Asperger's syndrome.

Life with my mother and father began in the great state of New York, and all five of us were born before we moved out of the tiny, two-bedroom apartment that they had moved into as soon as they were married. Mom stayed home with us while Dad worked to keep dinner on the table. We've always been happy to be a family because we loved each other and by the grace of God, we've never wanted for any of life's necessities.

Crystal and I are the oldest two children in my family. We were born eighteen months apart, and we have shared the same room, clothes, and experiences for the better part of our childhood. I don't remember anything about me before her birth, so I think it's fair to say that I would not be the woman I am today if I had not been Crystal's sister. She has served as one of the most powerful and persistent motivations for learning and growth in my life thus far.

Child number three is Elizabeth, who is another eighteen months or so younger than Crystal. She has been my best friend and partner-in-crime as well as my companion in pretend games ever since I can remember. She loves being with her family, making beautiful things, and figuring out how things work.

Next down is Mark, the only boy in the Brayton brood. He has masterfully fulfilled his masculine role as the nemesis of all of his sisters—and their precious dollies—since before he could talk. As a child, I would frequently beg my mother to send him back, but now that he's grown up, I wouldn't trade him for the world.

Then comes baby Jessica. She has the perfect personality for being the youngest. I was seven when she was born, so I have Jessica to thank for all my pre-babysitting experiences changing diapers, burping, testing bottles, and inventing age-appropriate baby games. I was older than I'd like to admit when I began seeing her as more of a sibling than a dependent, but I'm sure she always knew who her real mommy was.

Would you be willing to sit on my couch for a moment?

Take a good look at my family's entertainment center. There's a TV in the middle, flanked by two built-to-blast speakers Dad bought when he was in high school, with the radio/tape player and VCR stacked on top.

This entertainment center was custom designed and built by my father. See how he lined the widest parts with carpet to protect little children from hurting themselves as they toddle past? This man misses nothing. It's sturdy enough that a kid could ride his bike into the side of it, and nothing would come down. It's sturdy enough that when I was a child, I could climb up next to the speakers to put videos into the VCR on top. Mom often asked me to help her by doing this, and I was proud to be the only one of the kids who could.

This VCR fascinated me to no end when I was a child. I would peer inside the front flap of the VCR for as long as I could balance, trying to imagine what moved to make room for the video tape that I put in and which pieces pulled on the tape and set it into place. I even imagined that the different pieces were talking to each other—or to me. And sometimes I wondered whether anything else might fit in that perilous-looking space and survive coming out.

So begins the tale of the bologna sandwich.

I have never loved bologna, and I imagine it was indifference toward my lunch that provided the first threads for weaving this tale. One day, I tried to put a whole bologna sandwich into the VCR, and I remember the fear of realizing it wasn't going to come out.

I heard someone coming and jumped down. I sat on the couch, trying to look innocent, and wondered how long it would be before I was discovered. Then I imagined how I might respond to being asked about it. No one had witnessed my crime, but in the Brayton house, we all knew we would get in more trouble for lying about doing a wrong thing than for doing it. We also knew that telling the truth quickly improved our odds of receiving a more lenient consequence. More importantly, I loved my role as the trusted helper, and I had already promised myself I would never tell a lie; thus, I prepared to do the right thing and accept the consequences.

I didn't have to wait long for my opportunity. Dad came into the living room and immediately went over to look at the VCR. This surprised me, as I had somehow imagined that he might not have noticed until he went to use it next.

Visibly frustrated, he turned around and asked, "Who put bologna in the VCR?"

I took a deep breath. I opened my mouth to speak, and a little voice said, "I did!"

It wasn't mine.

I snapped my head toward the sound and saw Crystal smiling sweetly from her seat on the floor.

Not to be robbed of my heroic response, I said in my defense, "No, I did!"

In total disbelief, Dad looked from me to Crystal and back again a couple of times before he left the room without a word. We were both off the hook.

Disappointed that the story in my head had been changed without my consent and upset with her for uttering an untrue statement, I turned on Crystal with a full-blown lecture. Now I can see that her statement was probably just an opportunistic attempt to get an extra bologna sandwich, but at the time, I couldn't fathom why anyone would lie, especially when there was nothing to be gained by a successful deception. The fact that her statement had gotten me acquitted for my carelessness was completely lost on me, and the reason I was directing my apparently random outburst of frustration at

Crystal was completely lost on her. She left the experience cool, unconcerned, and indifferent. I left fuming, dissatisfied, and bewildered.

I had a piece of the puzzle, but the puzzle was growing.

✍

The puzzle that is my sister started puzzling before she learned to walk.

My dad remembers that the peculiarities of Crystal's life began early. As a baby, she would crawl over to the pile of shoes under the coat rack just inside the door and lick the bottoms of the shoes stored there. And since we lived where it's usually muddy if it isn't snowy, I'm sure there was plenty on those shoes to taste and enjoy. Of course, she was prevented from this practice as often as she was caught, but as any parent will tell you, you can't prevent a child from doing every unconscionable thing they are capable of conceiving to do. It's just not physically possible.

As she learned to walk, her ability to move forward developed much faster than her ability to stop. She didn't seem to grasp stopping or changing directions, so she would just walk until she ran into something stiff enough to knock her over, be it a person, a toy, or a wall.

My mom and dad both remember watching us play outside and having to help Crystal get up when she fell down. She would lose her balance, fall down, and then just look around at the rest of us with the same blithe expression she wore most of the time. She was apparently not anxious to rejoin the rest of us, so it made me wonder whether she wanted to get up or if she even wanted anything at all. Once she was reminded, she would get up and start playing again, but her expression never changed.

I have early memories of watching her trip and fall into the snow. Remembering how soggy and cold my snow pants would get if I sat down too long, I would get frustrated by the oblivious look on her face and order her to get up. Then I would feel bad because I knew Mom always used an encouraging tone when dealing with Crystal's snow-sitting, and I also knew that I really shouldn't be so impatient with her.

Crystal's behavior was so foreign to me that it confused and upset me. I truly wanted to be kind, but when I felt perplexed and out of control, I became so frustrated that I forgot to be kind. Consequently, the guilt from my unkindness and the irritation from being made to feel guilty swirled around and around inside me whenever I interacted with my sister. It was very uncomfortable.

It might have been easier to deal with if I could talk to her about it.

Crystal understood spoken English as early as you would expect any child to, but she didn't begin speaking "on time." I think she was about eighteen months old when someone began coming over once or twice a week to work with her on speech and other things. I was always a friendly and outgoing soul, so this person was naturally someone I wanted to meet, talk to, and play with. She did bring toys after all!

But in spite of all our protests, each time she came, Liz and I were babygated into the kitchen with instructions to color or draw or play with Play-Doh until Crystal was finished. I would lean over the baby gate as far as I could into the dining room and try to peek through the entryway and into the living room where they were. I caught glimpses of bright toys and smiling faces, and I wished I could play too.

Later, I would ask Mom what they did back there, and she would tell me they worked on her muscles and also showed her signs that she and Mom could both use to communicate. That wasn't what it looked like to me from what I could see through the entryway!

More seriously though, I remember sensing clearly that this was all very overwhelming for my mother. I also noticed, though I didn't understand why, that she wasn't as excited as I was to have Crystal's teacher come back again; however, Mom did teach Liz and me a few signs we could use with Crystal, which we enjoyed very much. I still remember "yes," "no," and "cookie" (what else does a kid need to know?). I also remember playing yes/no games with Crystal and my other siblings. Mom told us that Crystal could hear (I had never heard of sign language being used by anyone who wasn't deaf before) but that signing with her would help her learn how to communicate with her hands. And this, we all hoped, would help her learn to speak with her mouth someday.

I studied early childhood special education as an adult and learned that my sister would have been diagnosed with a "developmental delay" in order to have received these special services in our home. It is possible for more specific diagnoses to be given to children this young, but the professionals in this field understand the potentially long-lasting and negative effects of labeling a child as "disabled."

Many children who are treated for their delays before they even start school can learn past their challenges so well that they don't need much help once they reach kindergarten. In keeping with the law, a child must be diagnosed with *something* in order to qualify for receiving special services, but only one label is required.

It makes sense then that the best practice in early childhood intervention requires that interventionists assess each child carefully and then give the least intrusive diagnosis possible. For example, an eight-year-old child found to have autism and an "intellectual disability," which used to be termed even less flatteringly as "mental retardation," would likely have "autism" alone on their paperwork as the name of their disability. This would allow the specialists involved in his education and therapy to write interventions for both difficulties into his service plan without letting anyone else know that he had been diagnosed with another disability as well.

Before a child is old enough to go to school, it is very difficult to diagnose most disabilities correctly. Thankfully, advocates of the least intrusive practices worked until special education laws allowed for a more general diagnosis, "developmental delay," for children under three. And so, with a collective sigh of relief, early intervention practitioners all over the nation started diagnosing everything from stuttering to suspected autism as "developmental delay."

When Crystal was about eighteen months old, she was found eligible to receive a few different therapies at a little school down the road. Even though it was less than a ten-minute walking distance from my house, she rode to and from school every day on a little yellow school bus.

When I worked in the same building years later, there was a "Prospect Room," where all of the children had special needs and all of the teachers worked for the Prospect Child and Family Center, and the main Head Start classroom. The Prospect school had been established in the 1950s as the United Cerebral Palsy of Glens Falls by parents who wanted to help their children with disabilities in an age when there was little, if any, public support for it. At the other nearby and not-so-nearby Head Starts, they had "integrated" classrooms where children with special needs attended classes with other Head Start children and learned together. When Crystal attended, they called the site she went to the "CP Center."

But I learned all of this later. When she started going to school, all I knew was (1) my little sister got to start school before me, (2) she got to ride the cutest, smallest, *coolest* school bus I had ever seen, and (3) when I did start school, I would have to walk farther to school than she had to ride.

Don't they have room for me on there, too? It's just a little bit farther, I wondered. My mother explained it all to me, and I eventually accepted it as the way it would be and even should be, but I still pouted a little in my heart every time I walked in my snow pants and rainbow mittens past her school on the way to mine.

At some point, they had an open house at the Head Start building. All family members of the students were invited so that they could see what went on there, meet other students and their parents, and have a good time together. I was so excited that I was invited! I remember noticing as I walked in that the room was dimly lit, but Crystal looked like she felt so happy and safe there that I couldn't help but feel happy and safe too. They had a Chip and Dale movie on, offered everyone free doughnuts, sang some songs with us, and even taught us some new signs. I remember looking over at her sitting next to me and watching the movie, so enraptured and so in love with her life, and I honestly felt happy for her, no strings attached. I was happy at my school, and she was happy at hers, and that was enough.

After that, I was able to pass the school and think, "That's where Crystal goes to school. I wonder what they're doing now?" instead of pouting that I couldn't ride the little yellow bus.

But that didn't stop me from trying to convince Mom to let me ride from time to time.

So began my family's continuous contact with the world of special education. Crystal got help improving her speech for many years after those regular sessions in our little apartment. Once she started using words to speak around age three, it seemed like she immediately skipped to multi-syllable words and then complete sentences. As we like to joke in our family, it took her a while to start, but once she started talking, she never stopped!

∽ 2 ∾

Not Wrong, Just Different

I remember how exciting and almost magical picking out my first backpack and finding my name in my assigned cubby seemed to me. Starting kindergarten was more wonderful than I had ever imagined, but I learned more in school than just the letters of the alphabet. Over time, I also learned what "normal" was supposed to look like, and how difficult it would be for anyone, let alone Crystal, to live up to that ever illusive standard.

I admire my mother for working so hard to help us understand and enjoy Crystal when I know that she has endlessly puzzled over Crystal herself, wondering what to do with her.

As a child, Crystal had no imagination to speak of, so playtime was a frequent trial for all of us. When Elizabeth and I played together, I generally set the stage and gave out roles, and Elizabeth would sometimes refuse, negotiate, or suggest alternatives. We would choose pretty names for ourselves and imagine we lived in different time periods or regions of the world. Sometimes, we would leave an imaginary story game and come back to it later, but oftentimes, our characters and locations changed.

Crystal naturally wanted to play too because she could see how much fun we were having, but she struggled to keep track of the dynamic settings and dialogues. Another problem was that she hadn't really learned to pretend yet—she couldn't imagine being someone, somewhere, or something she wasn't in real life. We felt bad when we tried to exclude her, but in our immaturity, we didn't see any other option. The game had to continue, and it couldn't continue the way it needed to if we were tripping over her literal thinking every step of the way.

The scenario became sadly predictable. We told her she couldn't play, she went to tell Mom, and Mom brought Crystal back while holding her hand and told us that we had to let Crystal play too if we wanted to keep playing at all. She left it up to us to think up a way to involve Crystal without letting her ruin our game.

For someone who imagined things for fun all the time, I was woefully uncreative when faced with this impossibly daunting task. There was one time when I told her she was a beautiful statue in the palace and, as such, she was not allowed to move or talk. I felt horrible then, and it hurts my heart now every time I recall this story, but it's the truth.

As you might imagine, it wasn't long before this resulted in another tattle run to Mom. Our statue solution was not an acceptable alternative for my mother, but after telling us repeatedly to include Crystal with the same results, Mom decided to get creative.

I remember the first time she took Crystal into the kitchen to color and draw with her. By the time we wondered where Crystal was, she was already enjoying some one-on-one time with Mom. We discovered this new development from the dining room—on the other side of the baby gate. Of course we protested, but Mom simply replied that she was playing with Crystal because we would not.

I, for one, did not feel that this was an even trade because we had been entertaining ourselves in our pretend game, and Crystal was playing alone with Mom. I did not get to enjoy Mom's personal attention very often, and I *never* got to sit and color with her. I felt it was terribly unfair that Crystal was getting extra privileges just because she couldn't play make-believe, which wasn't even my fault; however, looking back, I think my mother was being *more* than fair to us.

Later on, Crystal did get a little better at make-believe, especially after I started integrating dress-up into our make-believe sessions when I discovered how to make a princess dress and cape combo out of belts and the quilts off our beds. But by then, she had learned how to read, so she generally preferred books to playing make-believe. An ultimate win for everyone, I guess.

By this time, she was very good at talking, but she would still mix up the meaning of words sometimes. For example, there was the time I asked her to get me a brush. She loved running little errands for people because she loved making us happy, so she skipped off to the bathroom and returned, grinning, with a comb. Surprised and disappointed—I despised combs as a child and couldn't imagine why any girl would use one—I explained the mix-up to her as kindly as I could, and she went back to switch it.

Ultimately, this interaction with her was positive, and we were both happier for it, so I chalked it up as a success. After this scene played out the same way a few times, however, I tried asking for a comb instead. It worked—she brought me a brush.

I was so pleased that I had figured this out all by myself until Mom discovered us. I still remember how my mom looked at me when she realized what was happening. We had a talk. Mom said she understood why I did it, but she needed me to help Crystal learn the correct words for things, not encourage her to practice using the wrong ones. We worked together to think of ways to teach Crystal the correct word for each item while still being able to send her on this mutually beneficial errand. She eventually learned, and we were all glad.

Another word Crystal struggled to understand was *sorry*.

Sorry is a useful word. When used properly, it can help heal hurt feelings and show that you know you were wrong and that you will try to do better in the future.

Sorry was an important concept for me. I have always considered it lying to say sorry before I felt sorry, so I refused to tell someone I was sorry unless I meant it. Sometimes, this philosophy got me stuck in time-out for disobeying my mother's instructions. While I felt this was unfair, part of me appreciated the time to cool down. If I hadn't felt that my sibling deserved whatever I did to them, I wouldn't have done it. So while I *wanted* to tell them I was sorry, I recognized that the anger I felt had to go away before I could say sorry.

When Crystal said sorry, it meant something different.

For example, if I was fighting with Liz over something and Crystal walked by, she would tell me, "Sorry." In those moments, all the negativity in my system would instantly refocus onto her. My mind would explode with urgency as I jumped into the suddenly vital task of convincing her that telling someone sorry for something she had nothing to do with did not mean anything, nor did it help anyone. I doubted Crystal heard a word of it because she would just look at me with a surprised expression on her face, wishing her attempt at diffusing the stressful anger had been as successful in real life as it had in her mind.

The way she used this word to apologize for something upsetting she *had* done was also bizarre to me. She would say "sorry" the instant our eyebrows furrowed or our smile turned into a frown, sometimes even before she understood what she had done to upset us. It seemed clear that her goal was to spit the word out before we had a chance to speak. She got really quick at it, as if she were drawing her sword for a duel.

What really puzzled me was how sure she seemed that "sorry" was a magic force field against negative feelings. For instance, I would sometimes walk into a room where she was doing something that she knew was against the rules, and I would hear "sorry" and see an oh-no-I-just-got-caught-so-now-I-have-to-stop look in the same moment.

That always felt like a lie to me.

Young as I was, I knew in my mind that I had to think about whether I was sorry before I could honestly make that little one-word commitment. I also understood that I couldn't have the same feelings in my heart when I did something wrong that I had when I said I was sorry for doing it. Being the benevolent older sister that I was, I became intent on making sure my younger sister had an accurate grasp of the reality that surrounded her and permeated the rest of our lives, so I explained to her that "sorry" meant you felt bad about what you did and that you wouldn't do it again.

I eventually felt the need to add to my definition the observation that while she might have been sorry that she got caught doing something wrong, it was better to say sorry when she actually felt bad for what she did or at least for hurting the other person's feelings. Mom, Liz, and even Dad tried to help her understand this concept, but our frustration only grew as time went on with no real sign of improvement or even solid comprehension.

As I puzzled over her strange behavior, I ultimately realized that Crystal thought "sorry" was a magic button that people pushed to help others feel better. That result was what she observed and what she wanted to receive, so whenever the heat of contention was too hot for her to handle, she would just press the magic button. I imagine she was really frustrated when this method often proved to be counterproductive.

Telling the story this way makes it sound like she was pretty slow on the uptake. In reality, she actually learned her lessons quickly, just not the lessons we were trying to teach. As is true for many of us, Crystal often tended to be much more willing to shape what she naturally did and felt into more socially acceptable forms than to actually change her behavior and perspectives to meet a higher standard. Eventually, "sorry" almost completely disappeared from Crystal's vocabulary, but it was replaced with other words that more subtly served the same purpose—to get people to feel better without actually changing a thing.

Another concept we struggled to help Crystal understand was why big girls shouldn't suck their thumbs.

At the start, Crystal's thumb-sucking habit was admittedly very cute. It was a picture someone might paint and hang up on the wall: a little girl with fair skin and raven hair, twirling her beautiful curls with one hand while she sucks the thumb of the other.

Although health professionals wouldn't want children much older than babies to suck their thumbs because of the associated effects that thumb sucking may have on them later in life, everyday people generally accept the fact that it is simply a phase some people go through; however, most of these same people don't expect this habit to continue on throughout childhood and certainly not into adolescence.

It wasn't that my parents weren't aware of the risks, or that they didn't try to stop Crystal's thumb sucking. As the years passed, we had to continuously remind her to take her thumb out of her mouth "because you're not a baby anymore." I remember pulling her thumb out of her mouth, and I remember how quickly she learned to watch for it and resist me with all of her strength when I tried. My parents worried that it was interfering with her language acquisition and the correct development of her mouth and teeth; however, while it was easy to list the reasons why a person should not suck her thumb, it was much more difficult to find and implement a long-term solution.

One theory was that if we could determine when she did it the most, we might find that these were times when she felt insecure and in need of comfort. Then we could teach her healthier coping strategies. So we all paid attention and discovered that she only sucked her thumb when she was bored, which she seemed to be on an almost perpetual basis. As far as we could tell, she didn't suck her thumb when she was sad, frightened, or ill at ease, but she never seemed to experience any of these emotions at all! What coping strategies does a person need for boredom?

Mom and I got so exhaustingly persistent that she finally stopped, or so we thought. We soon discovered that she only abstained when she suspected that we could see her, which was even more frustrating for us because we could see that she had the power to curb her habit but no internal motivation to do so, at least beyond a desire to avoid being chewed out.

Other children we knew teased her about it sometimes, but she could not be deterred. She twirled her hair into terrible knots and sucked on her thumb until it looked like a bleached raisin. Her hand and mouth smelled like dried spit all the time, and her thumb knuckle would chap around the base in the winter. Gross!

There was this one time when we went to Grandpa's farm to help him plant strawberry seeds. Dad took his little brother, all of the children, and a wheelbarrow filled with hundreds of little pink seeds out to the back field for us to plant by hand.

It sounds like the perfect setting for happy family memories destined to be shared over mugs of hot cocoa at family gatherings for years to come, but that's not how it turned out for me.

Before we began planting, Dad gave us a brief orientation. He showed us how to plant the seeds, and he warned us to keep our hands away from our mouths while we planted because the seeds were poisonous. I was a little surprised that we were being allowed to handle something poisonous. After all, I watched Looney Tunes all the time, so I knew that anyone who swallowed something poisonous would instantly die.

Scenes from that show played in my mind as I watched Crystal to see if the peril of death was enough to temper her insatiable habit. No such luck. She just slid along, planted a few seeds, stopped to suck the dirt off her thumb, took a few more steps, and planted a few more seeds until she ran out and had to get more from the wheelbarrow. My frenzied mind looked to Dad to save her. He saw what Crystal was doing and tried to convince her not to, but she simply ignored his counsel, without a word of defense or sign of rebellious intent in her eyes, and continued calmly on her way.

I was very upset with my father for allowing her to continue planting and sucking her thumb, and I was afraid that she might get sick and fall over at any moment. I went to inform him that she had never stopped, but when I came over to where he was working with my uncle Dan, I heard them joking about different things that might happen to her as a result of her stubbornness.

Dad ignored me. Maybe he didn't hear me—I found out much later that he was actually in the habit of tuning my voice out because I complained about things so often. At the time, I was so upset that I cried. I tried to convince Crystal to at least use her other hand to plant if she couldn't stop sucking her thumb, and all the while, my uncle went on laughing about how ridiculous Crystal looked plodding along and sucking her dirty thumb. Crystal just kept going and going and going like the big pink bunny from the Energizer commercial, expressionless and oblivious to the impending doom looming above her pretty dark-haired head.

I was sure my sister was going to get sick and die and that no one cared but me, and I wasn't able to fully get over what I felt that day until many years later. Still, something deep down in my soul wouldn't let me believe that my father would actually let Crystal die because she wouldn't stop sucking her thumb. I wondered if he had made up the poisonous seed thing to motivate Crystal to keep her dirt-covered hands out of her mouth. Or maybe he wasn't sure if they were poisonous, and he was willing to risk it since no one seemed to be suffering any ill effects. Finally, as an adult, I discovered that while store-bought seeds are frequently treated with chemicals, strawberry seeds are not inherently poisonous.

Judging by how clearly I could see the social and physical repercussions of Crystal's thumb-sucking habit, you would think I would have no interest in adopting the practice myself. But I could also clearly see some benefits. For example, it never failed to get her attention, and I thought there must be something to it if she was so intent on doing it even with everyone dogging her about it all the time. So I stuck my thumb in my mouth and tried to suck it.

I must be doing it wrong, I thought. *Maybe it's not far enough in my mouth or maybe too far.* I looked at how Crystal was doing it, and it looked like I was doing it right. It just seemed so uncomfortable.

Maybe it's a thumbnail problem. I didn't like how my thumbnail scratched my tongue when I did it. So I clipped that nail, but then it hurt because I clipped it too short.

Mom said something about Crystal's thumb being soft. Maybe I have to keep at it until mine's the right shape. I sucked softly, and then so hard I made my mouth sore. Nothing helped. I gave it an honest try, but I ultimately decided that it was no fun for me.

I'm sorry to say that my experiment didn't make me more merciful or understanding. On the contrary, I simply added "it doesn't even taste like anything" and "isn't it uncomfortable?" to my list of reasons why she should give it up.

I didn't give up though. If there was no benefit to sucking my thumb, there was still attention to be gotten by doing it. Around the same time I was working through this conundrum, I happened across a group of my class-mates at school who were showing each other how to act like they were suck-ing their thumbs without actually doing it. I eagerly learned this new skill and had it down in no time.

After school, I tried to hide my pleasure and anticipation as I folded my thumb down into my palm, wrapped my other fingers around it, brought my thumb knuckle up to my lips, and made sucking noises. It did get me attention, but Mom looked so upset and perplexed when she saw me that I decided to show her what I was doing.

It was hard for her to decide what to say after that. It ended up being something about how I needed to be a good example. So at my next oppor-tunity, I encouraged Crystal to do it my way instead. It was cleaner and better for her mouth, I told her, and she could even enjoy the undeniable benefit of knowing something the other person didn't know. I told her she could even suck on her thumb knuckle while she got used to the switch. It seemed like the perfect solution to me, but she remained unconvinced.

I guess we never could persuade her to do anything, but we knew that wasn't because she wasn't smart enough to understand.

My grandparents liked to say that once Crystal started to talk, she skipped from the normal first words to multi-syllable words and onto com-plete sentences in no time at all. After that, we wondered sometimes how to get her to stop talking or at least how to keep her from saying certain things we found odd, rude, or otherwise embarrassing.

Did she wait so long to talk because she had so much to say that she wasn't sure how best to say it? Was she content with just listening, or was she waiting to get it just right? Whatever it was, we learned quickly that her rapidly growing vocabulary was nothing short of astounding, as was her memory.

We also puzzled over how the things she considered important enough to remember were different from the things most people would remember.

After her first day of kindergarten, she told us about some of the people she had met. This alone would not have seemed unusual, but what surprised us was how many people she had remembered and that she could recall both their first and last names. She told us how she had played with Amy Goodrich at the blocks, sat next to Ruth Owens at lunch, and about how Robby Baldwin was mean to her.

After my first day, I could only ever remember the names of people I knew from the year before, plus an outstanding new kid or two and any-one else named Ashley. Consequently, as I listened to her excited and very detailed description of her day, I felt a bit jealous, even a little defensive, as if I didn't measure up somehow.

It took us a few weeks to convince her that she didn't have to refer to peo-ple by both of their names every time and that people usually found it odd, especially in such a casual setting as school. Looking back, I don't know why it was so important to us in the first place. What was wrong with it, anyway? It was odd, yes, but it was certainly not harmful, hurtful, or even ignorant sounding. In fact, many adults work hard at memorizing the first and last names of people they meet.

It is much easier for me to see this as a gift now, but at the time it was so alarming and out of the ordinary that Mom and I did the best we could to reform her behavior. It seems that we spent a lot of time and emotional energy working to conform her to norms whenever possible, especially since so many of the odd things about Crystal were unconformable. This time, we eventually succeeded, and she switched to using first names only when she talked about her classmates. I imagine that what we tried to teach her was reinforced enough at school that she ultimately decided we were telling her the truth.

Now I wonder if we actually failed Crystal those few times we thought we succeeded.

One of the silly things Crystal did was eat some foods from top to bottom that most of us would eat from side to side. Hamburgers were a prime example. Her eyes showed both excitement and concentration as she peeled the bun off the burger one layer at a time with her fingers. She then ate any cheese and removed any offending vegetables that might stand between her and the ketchup, which she would then wipe off the top of the meat, licking one finger-full at a time until she couldn't get any more off. Next, she pinched pieces off the hamburger patty if it was soft enough, or just tore it into pieces if it wasn't, and ate that one piece at a time as well. She dealt with the bottom bun in the same way as the top bun, and at last, she was finished. She ate pizzas similarly, only ever touching the food with her fingertips.

It didn't bother me much when she picked off toppings, but watching her lick stuff off her fingers was really unappetizing. If I had licked my fingers at the table, I would have been told not to because "that's what napkins are for."

At first, my parents tried to get her to eat the same way as the rest of us, but they ultimately changed their approach. They decided it wasn't actually wrong, or even important enough to add to the already long list of things we told her she couldn't do on a regular basis.

After that, if any of us gave her any grief for eating "weird," my mom would remind us, "Different isn't always wrong." I really did want to be accepting and charitable, even though I often had a hard time with this, so I tried to mentally ignore her and push the feelings of disgust away. I did my best to remind myself that there were some things about Crystal I would just have to learn to accept. I could love her anyway, and that was OK.

We all found it especially odd that Crystal wouldn't eat hot dogs. I could understand carrots, peas, and green beans (I didn't like any of those things either), but hot dogs seemed a little strange. She absolutely refused to eat them.

I didn't like hot dogs much either, and I really liked hamburgers, which Mom always gave Crystal whenever the rest of us got hot dogs on macaroni and cheese dinner nights. Whenever I complained of unfair treatment, Mom would explain that she wasn't going to force Crystal to eat something that wasn't that great for her anyway.

Aren't hamburgers better for me, too, then? I wondered.

Mom would go on to say that I didn't get a hamburger too because I would eat a hot dog if that's all there was. My other siblings thought it wasn't fair that they didn't get a hamburger, but had they been given the choice between the two, they would have chosen a hot dog anyway. All this left me feeling as if Crystal was being rewarded for being stubborn and I was being punished because I didn't have it in me to boycott a food I only kind of didn't like. To be fair, we did all have hamburgers for dinner from time to time, but for me, hamburgers and hot dogs always made me think of how unfair my life was.

The apartment I grew up in was actually the downstairs of an old house my great-great-grandfather Whitman built himself many years before. My great-grandma Taylor, his daughter, lived in the upstairs apartment, now only accessible by an outdoor staircase, and my parents rented the down-stairs apartment from her.

She loved to have us come visit, and we loved to visit her. Several times a week, Mom gave me permission to go up by myself or to take either Crystal or Elizabeth with me.

Grandma Taylor came with her own set of rules. These were the kind of rules you were either warned about by your parents or learned from your own uncomfortable experiences, not the kind that would be posted on the wall somewhere for easy reference.

Her most important rule was to be quiet—play quietly, look through magazines quietly, eat delicious cinnamon and sugar apple slices quietly, watch TV quietly. Silence was not required, but we needed to interact with each other quietly, considerately, and without any fighting. This was a generally welcome change from the usual, and there were plenty of fun, quiet things to do at Grandma's house. We played dominoes with her, rearranged the little balls of her Chinese chess set into pretty patterns, peeked at the treasures in her mysterious closets, talked about what we were doing in school, dressed the Barbies she had handmade clothing for, listened to stories from when she was younger, sang for her, and flipped through magazines with pretty pictures of porcelain dolls and snow globes. Sometimes, she would drop off to sleep in her chair, and we would just find something to do that wouldn't wake her until she rejoined us. I really enjoyed spending time with her most of the time.

The other major rule was that we were to gratefully eat whatever she chose to feed us until it was gone. Elizabeth and I were a team when boiled eggs were on the menu. Liz only liked the yellows and I only liked the whites, so we ate each other's so that nothing was wasted and no one got in trouble. I knew not to complain about the food Grandma Taylor gave me either, even if it was vegetables. Crystal learned this rule the hard way and obeyed it strictly ever since.

I always felt proud of her for saying "thank you" for foods she would complain about having to eat at home. I was especially proud of her one day when Grandma Taylor served us hot dogs for a snack, and Crystal ate them all up without a word of complaint. I was so surprised and so pleased that I told Grandma about it. I still remember the sound of my high voice as I praised my sister for eating all her food without complaining, even though she didn't like it. I also remember the surprise and disappointment that descended on my little heart when Grandma's face changed. She scolded Crystal for not telling her that she didn't like hot dogs until Grandma got so worked up that she sent us home.

I was so sad and so sorry! I thought it was great that Crystal had made that sacrifice to be a good guest, and I felt terrible that I had made it a waste by telling the truth. Crystal wasn't mad at me, but she was very upset. I tried to console her by telling her that she hadn't done anything wrong and that it wasn't nice for Grandma to treat her that way. I also told her how sorry I was for making Grandma angry with her.

When I told Mom what happened, she just rolled her eyes in Grandma Taylor's general direction and reassured Crystal she wasn't in trouble anymore and that she could play at home and be happy.

Grandma at the Farm, who was Grandma Taylor's daughter, remembers, "Looking back, I think Crystal made Grandma Taylor uneasy in some ways. A lot of people felt that way because they didn't see her all the time. People always assume that people who did certain things had certain motivations, but with Crystal, it was always a little difficult to tell, even if you asked her, what her real motivation for anything was."

As I got older, I began to wonder whether Grandma Taylor was so thrown off by Crystal's oddities partly because she had some form of Asperger's herself. Maybe someday we'll find out.

I know now that my sister was diagnosed and given an IEP in about second or third grade, but I wasn't aware of that then. What I did understand was that Crystal went to the "Resource Room" sometimes to get extra help and that she really liked it there.

And why wouldn't she? The teachers there were very nice to me and the other kids whenever we ran across them. They worked at the end of the hall where I had my class in second grade, so sometimes I would peek in on our way out to recess or just because. They had exercise balls and all kinds of other fun stuff in there. I wanted to go play too, but whenever I asked an adult about it, they would tell me it might look like they were playing, but to the kids in Resource, it was work like the work I had to do in school.

The other kids who went to Resource didn't seem to have the same kinds of needs as Crystal. One girl wore a helmet, and I saw her in the cafeteria sometimes doing exercises on the ball. One boy joined my class in fourth grade, and he had a really cool motorized wheelchair that he would let me ride on sometimes when the teachers weren't looking. Maybe my second grade boyfriend went there too. Kids made fun of him for talking slow, but I thought he was awesome.

I really never had much of a problem with people with special needs. In fact, I usually enjoyed being around them. I had fun helping them feel like equals—because they were—and like they had a friend—because they did. I know now that the word *fair* doesn't mean treating everyone the same; it means loving everyone—really loving them and not just saying so—and giving them what they *need*.

There was a song I loved to sing in church that really gave voice to my feelings about all of these people. It's called "I'll Walk with You":

If you don't walk as most people do,
Some people walk away from you,
But I won't! I won't!
If you don't talk as most people do,
Some people talk and laugh at you,
But I won't! I won't!
I'll walk with you. I'll talk with you.
That's how I'll show my love for you.
Jesus walked away from none.
He gave his love to ev'ryone.
So I will! I will!
Jesus blessed all he could see,
Then turned and said, "Come, follow me."
And I will! I will!
I will! I will!
I'll walk with you. I'll talk with you.
That's how I'll show my love for you.

I always felt something special inside when I sang that song, something I have come to identify as the spirit of God. Now is as good a time as any to state my beliefs clearly because it will help you understand my story as well as why I feel every person has the inalienable right of believing what they will believe for themselves.

I believe there is literally a God in Heaven who loves and cares about His children and that He knows us each by name and pays attention to us on a personal level. I also believe He wants to communicate that love to us and that He chooses moments when we are particularly close to Him to let us know He loves us and is pleased with what we're doing. He does this by sending the Holy Ghost, the same spirit that appeared as a dove when Jesus was baptized and the Father announced Jesus for all to hear. That same Holy Spirit speaks to us too, and if we listen, it's there for each of us to hear. It is that spirit I feel when I sing about loving others who are different from myself. You have probably felt something similarly special, a happy, secure, peaceful feeling that comes when you know you're doing something right, and I believe that feeling comes because you've made your Maker proud. I try to live in such a way that I make Him happy as often as possible.

When I sang that song, I meant every word, and I tried to live my life so that would always be true. And I know God was pleased with me for it because of that spirit I felt when I sang it.

I have always loved singing. One of the things I loved most about school was Mrs. Mitchell, our music teacher, and the music programs we prepared and performed for every major holiday. First and third grade were especially exciting because those grades got to be part of a musical Christmas play.

For my first grade play, I practiced diligently for my role as Elf #3 in "The Littlest Christmas Tree." This role required me to step forward and say my line two times during the play and sing all of the songs with the rest of my class. I remember the two big red dots of make-up I wore on my cheeks, which matched the other elves', and the maroon and white dress I wore because I didn't have a red or green one.

In my third grade play, I was Bell #4, the only supporting character in the play that also sang a solo. I was so honored and excited that Mrs. Mitchell chose me to fill that special role. My dad videotaped the whole play, and Mom told me that he'd been so proud of me that he cried during my solo. These successes brought happiness and pride to my little heart, but my heart also had to work through a little sadness every time I was not given the starring role.

In Crystal's kindergarten year, Mrs. Mitchell did a non-Christmas play with them. Mrs. Kenyon, the kindergarten teacher, and Mrs. Mitchell put their heads together and decided to cast my sister for the lead role.

When Crystal bounded through the door to tell us she was going to be the Little Red Hen, I couldn't believe my ears.

I knew it wasn't kind to feel the way I felt, so I asked Mom about it in a more private setting. Why did Crystal, who couldn't pretend and couldn't sing, get the star role of her play, while I was the master of both and only got minor roles in mine?

I am grateful my mom was willing to listen and not reprove me for my feelings. Mom calmly reminded me that not everyone could have a starring role, and she explained to me that I needed to let this be Crystal's chance to shine. Mrs. Kenyon and Mrs. Mitchell had talked to my mom and said they felt that Crystal could do it, which touched Mom deeply. Mom asked me to think about it from Crystal's perspective as someone who is constantly made to feel like she falls short, and she encouraged me to try to be proud of Crystal. I knew Mom was right, but in my egocentricity, I still felt it was unjust that Crystal had been granted a privilege that I had been denied, even though I was clearly more talented.

I'll learn, though. Don't worry. Charity comes with time—and practice.

In the meantime, my role as older sister was beginning to change.

One day at school, a child I had never seen before stopped me in the hallway and asked with sincerity and concern in her voice, "Not to be mean, but is your sister retarded?"

My mind exploded, and my world changed instantly. I realized with unexpected and undesired clarity how Crystal was perceived by those around her. I also realized that it was up to me, in this moment and always, to defend her and acquaint people with the truth.

My mom would have been proud of my answer because it was the same she had given me when I asked her the same question: "No, she just learns differently than most people do." The girl seemed satisfied and went to class. She had no idea what her question had done.

From then on, I have cringed every time I heard that word. At that time, "retarded" was one of the big adjectives to use in school, possibly for its shock value. Later on, when I was in middle and high school, its meaning changed from the more accurate one I understood and became synonymous with "unfair," "boring," "uncomfortable," "dumb," or any other adjective that described something the person didn't want to have to deal with. It was a great catch-all, the antithesis of "nice," but I never could tolerate this use of the word, no matter how many times my friends have teased me to "lighten up" about it. To me, the word has always been serious, and it was always meant to describe an actual condition that affects people and their families in real and almost tangible ways.

No, Crystal was not retarded. Retarded literally means "slowed down" (imagine my concern at being told to "ritard" in music class), but to my peers, it really meant "stupid." Crystal was slowed down socially, even mentally in some areas, but she certainly was not—is not—stupid.

The mental challenges associated with Crystal's disability haven't been anywhere near as difficult for me to handle as the social ones anyway.

There was a person who entered Crystal's life when Crystal was in about second grade whom I'll call Corrinne. She was a sour-faced bully, but Crystal adored her. Recesses were arranged so that only two grade levels were out at a time, so I never saw Elizabeth, but Elizabeth and I both saw Crystal.

We noticed that Corrinne didn't like it if Crystal played with us or anyone else, and she would snobbishly command that Crystal walk away from us with her, and Crystal would always comply. Crystal followed Corrinne around wherever she went and did Corrinne's bidding all day. Corrinne would ask Crystal to do mean things such as "don't play with her," or "ignore her," or "walk with me instead of your sister." She would even call Crystal some name or tell her to lie.

At home, Mom and I tried to talk to Crystal about it. *She is not a friend. She is a bully. Does she ever do nice things for you? Why don't you tell her that what she tells you to do is wrong? She's not your boss, she can't "make" you do anything, so stop saying that she "makes" you do things.*

Crystal would always answer that if she didn't comply, Corrinne would say she wouldn't be Crystal's friend anymore. My thought was, *Great! Problem solved!* But Crystal didn't feel the same way.

"She's my best friend!" she would pout.

"Find a better best friend," I would almost shout.

That always ended the conversation, but she never changed her mind.

Thus began her first abusive relationship; she was addicted to a person and a relationship with someone who used her as a puppet. This puppet was willing and loyal, just as long as the puppeteer remained her consistent and predictable companion.

I could see that Crystal saw the price of being made uncomfortable sometimes as being very small compared to her reward—a friend who would always be there to give her attention. It was as if she really didn't believe that there were better friends out there to be had. At the time, I thought maybe everyone else was mean to her, but it turned out they weren't. Maybe Crystal just didn't want a best friend she had to share.

We knew Corrine was bad news, but we didn't realize how much control she had over Crystal until after Elizabeth started kindergarten. Crystal was only one grade level ahead of Liz, so they shared the playground for part of recess. One day, Liz ran home almost in tears to tell Mom a story it still hurts me to recall. Liz had greeted Crystal during recess and invited her to play, and Corrinne told Crystal to call Liz a "noodle head." Crystal promptly obeyed, then walked away as commanded without an ounce of apology on her face.

Even as young as Liz and I were, we realized it was a super immature and uncreative name to call someone, which made it particularly insulting. It was hard for Elizabeth to verbalize all of the emotions that experience made her feel, but we understood. I felt like I had been there too, almost right with her somehow.

When Crystal was questioned, her responses were the same as ever. She didn't ever seem to grasp why all of us were so upset about it.

This incident really cut me deeply. I was sure she was slipping out of our grasp as this evil influence increased its hold on her, and it was too much for me to handle. Young children experience and suffer sorrow in real ways—ways the adults around them can only try to understand.

In my sorrow, I wrote a poem I wish I still had. It didn't rhyme the way I wanted it to, but it conveyed the helplessness I felt, and the special kind of sadness that came from trying to help someone who didn't want help. My writing gave voice to the feelings that were too big for my heart to hold alone. I was still sad, but getting it out did help me feel better.

I would like to say that Crystal learned her lesson and that this was the last bully she would commit her friendship to, but I promised to be honest. This relationship was actually the first of many. The crazy thing was that most, if not all, of these relationships were much more painful for the family who loved her to witness than for her to participate in.

Many, many years later, Crystal and other members of my family were helping me with a garage sale in front of our old apartment when a familiar face came to look at what we were selling. It was Corrinne. She was taller and prettier and not so pinch-faced, but still unwelcome in my family space as far as I was concerned.

It took Crystal a minute to register her face, but she finally recognized her long-lost friend and ran to her, fully expecting a happy reunion. Corrinne was very kind and polite, though surprised and a little uncomfortable. I doubted she remembered Crystal at all, but she said she did just because it obviously meant a great deal to Crystal.

Crystal gave her a big hug and tried to reminisce about old times. But third grade was at least ten years removed from Corrinne's memory by this time, and while Corrinne had meant a lot to Crystal, I don't know whether Crystal meant enough to Corrinne to make her memorable.

At any rate, long after Corrinne and her dad drove away, Crystal was still giggling and chatting about how glad she was to run into Corrinne again and catch up, and the rest of us were still looking at each other in disbelief that, even all these years later, Crystal honestly thought Corrinne had been her friend.

When Crystal was still young, she would insist on hugging anyone who was hurt. I think seeing someone upset made her wish someone would hug her so she would feel better, so she assumed the person hurt would be grateful to receive the same treatment. With some trial and error and lots of practice, we helped her learn to first ask whether the hurt person wanted a hug instead of just giving them one. She also learned that sometimes people who weren't hurt didn't want hugs, and that was a wish that needed to be respected in order for people to be happy with her. She gave a little and we gave a little. She learned not to hug us all the time, and we learned to let her hug us sometimes when we didn't really want a hug just to make her happy. Sometimes these hugs even had the desired effect of making us both happier.

These were the first of many hug-related rules that Crystal had to follow. The most exhaustive list of rules applied specifically to giving hugs at church. Crystal generally didn't give hugs to strangers at the grocery store or the post office, but she felt so good at church and was so happy to see all the people there that she just hugged everybody. She would hug anyone, especially adults, and sometimes multiple times. This was embarrassing and awkward for us and, I imagine, for some of the people she hugged. On the other hand, hugging people wasn't an inherently bad thing, so it didn't feel right to just tell her to stop.

With some direct instructions and a little practice, Crystal came to understand that she could only hug people she personally knew and only once per Sunday. A couple of exceptions were made for members of the congregation who specifically requested hugs or expressed that they would like to have as many hugs as Crystal had to give, which actually surprised me.

How kind these people are! I thought. Originally, I figured they enjoyed her hugs better because they only occurred once a week, but eventually, I decided that I could choose to enjoy her hugs, too. I also determined to cut her some slack and let her hug me more often than I did already, especially when she asked me first.

Mom also had her own set of rules. Mom didn't like to be hugged from behind or around the neck, and she didn't like the big, sloppy kisses that generally accompanied the hugs. The rest of us decided to adopt these rules too, so Crystal always had to ask before giving kisses, and she also had to wait for us to turn around before hugging us.

All of the rules grew and changed with Crystal. As she grew older, the church rule of only hugging *people* she knew eventually morphed to only hugging *women* she knew, with a few specific exceptions.

But there were other problems too. For example, she always squeezed really hard. I imagine that in her mind, she was expressing how enthusiastically happy she was to see someone. When she was four or five, it wasn't a big deal, but at twelve or thirteen, she sometimes hurt people. Hence the rule was implemented that she was not allowed to squeeze hard or hold on too long, and she was *never* allowed to pick someone up off the ground. This set of rules was particularly important when it came to hugging boys and children.

I would like to hope she learned some of the whys and the hows and the what fors behind the rules, but I think it's more likely that she just programmed them into the operating system in her brain and never assigned more meaning to them than that.

$$\mathscr{D}$$

Every girl I know of has had an irrational crush on someone they had no real hope of actually meeting, much less dating, at some point in her life. It's something that everyone has dealt with and something that some of us have struggled to get over. One of the things that Crystal and I had in common as children was our crush on Michael Jackson. We watched his music videos on TV and Free Willy over and over again, sharing admiring smiles and giggles as we danced and sang along.

I also developed a crush on Jonathan Taylor Thomas, better known as "JTT," after I went to a friend's house and saw her cute poster of him. He was especially popular then because of his role in *The Lion King*, and I realized even at the time that this was a silly reason to like someone. It just seemed like it was important to like someone famous, so I picked him as my favorite. Crystal, though, had a crush on Gaston from *Beauty and the Beast*. Not the voice actor who played him, the animated character.

This puzzled and frustrated me to no end.

I tried to tell her that he wasn't real because he was a cartoon character and that he didn't actually exist. And he's gross! *And* he's the bad guy! While she never contested their validity, none of these facts diminished her devotion in the slightest. No matter what I said, she would simply restate that he was the most handsome man ever and that she was going to marry him someday.

In a way, her crush on Gaston foreshadowed her future unhealthy relationships.

She told me as an adult that looks didn't matter to her, but I have often wondered whether she said it because I used to say it back in high school and it sounded right to her, or because she really meant it. She has "fallen in like" with some pretty unattractive people before, several of whom she also dated, so it could be that she didn't see looks as an important criterion. On the flip side, maybe Gaston was her favorite less because of his looks and more because of his deep, powerful singing voice.

Who knows? I hope that she'll prove me wrong someday.

When we lived in New York, we were just down the street from the community pool, which was free for locals. We tried to go there occasionally, but there were so many people, and I was such a big scaredy-cat that we usually opted to drive a little farther and swim at Grandma's house instead; however, Crystal and I did go for swimming lessons.

When she was six and I was eight, Crystal and I began swimming lessons together. I liked to swim my way. I would play around in the shallow end, dunking my head down and flipping my long hair up out of the water like Ariel from *The Little Mermaid*. But as hard as I tried, I couldn't imagine the reason behind dropping from a standing position straight down into the water so the chlorinated water could sting my nose. I had never seen anyone do that before, but it was one of the first required exercises in the course.

Everyone from the instructors to my mother (an avid swimmer and diver) to well-meaning friends and strangers told me to "just blow out of your nose as you go down," but it just never worked for me. After enduring several classes that included this torture session, I was frustrated that I couldn't do it, upset that no one could come up with a different solution for me to try, maddened by the pain I experienced every time I went under, and convinced that I wouldn't move on to the intermediate level if I wasn't ultimately successful.

So I cheated.

I dropped down and then, at the last possible moment, tipped my head forward so my forehead hit at the same time as my nose. This gave me the tiny bit of whatever I was missing that I needed. In my memory, I jumped up out of the water cheering, "I did it! It didn't sting!" with a smile so big that it was goofy, and the instructor for my skill group, who of course couldn't have missed such an obvious modification to the prescribed procedure, half-rolled her eyes and waved me on to the group working on the next skill.

Of course, Crystal had it down the first or second time she tried, and she was already partway around the rotation and well on her way to mastering all of the beginner skills.

As we moved forward, we would also go to my grandma's pool to play together with the rest of the family. It was hard for me to hear Mom praise Crystal's skills when I still couldn't doggy paddle. That's not to say Crystal was very good at swimming, but she just wasn't afraid to try. I tried to do what she did, but I gave up almost instantly because I knew I wasn't doing it right.

Her fearlessness, however, did not come without a downside.

As soon as we began swimming lessons but long before she knew how to swim, Crystal's time swimming at Grandma's pool started looking different. Several times per visit, she would wordlessly walk over to the deep end, jump in, and then tread water until someone came and rescued her. My uncles would laugh at her, but she showed no evidence of shame. Elizabeth and I would yell that she should stay with us in the shallow end and not do dangerous things, but she didn't look at us or respond. It seemed like she was acting without feeling. I wonder how much time she spent—or even spends—feeling.

Eventually, someone would kindly remind her that she should tell people that she was going to jump in because she couldn't really swim yet, and she would nod her head. Then she would splash or doggy-paddle around for a little longer, get out, and jump in again with the same result.

I knew it was a ridiculous thing to do, and I wondered why she didn't learn, but I still wished that I wasn't too afraid to do the same thing.

In swimming class, she moved fearlessly and effortlessly through all the requirements, and I lurched along, resisting every step of progress that needed to be made. I wished my mom would stay and watch because then it would be easier to trust the instructor to hold me up while I tried to reach and kick at the same time and to trust the instructor to know not to let me go until I was ready.

It's amazing to me how many details I remember from that trial in my little life. I didn't want to quit even though I struggled to trust these people I didn't know, especially since I had learned from previous experiences that they weren't as interested in taking my concerns as seriously as I would have liked them to.

If my mother had been there—or if I had had more warning—I might have been able to pass the "big test." I might have been able to jump into the deep end without plugging my nose, and one of the instructors could have grabbed me and helped me to the ladder so I could climb out of the pool.

I had the first turn, but I couldn't do it, so I watched every other child in the class jump into the pool while I tried to talk myself into it. The instructors were kind and patient, and I can still remember the smiling face of the tan young man who stood in the water, reaching up to catch me, but I couldn't jump. I also couldn't imagine what would happen. I didn't think I would drown, but I wasn't sure how fast I could get out again if I stung my nose, or what he would do if I jumped so far away from him that he would have to move to get me, or even whether it would hurt me under my arms if I jumped just right for him to catch me.

I just couldn't jump. I was so disappointed.

Mom told me that she and the instructors agreed that even though I could pass without passing the final test, I should probably take the beginner level again so that I could gain confidence and improve my skills. Crystal, however, would be moving onto the intermediate level. I was not surprised, and though I was disappointed that my little sister was moving on without me, I could see that it was probably for the best. The thought about moving onto the intermediate level intimidated me a little anyway.

The hardest part for me was coming to terms with the fact that, for the first time in my life, I wasn't better than Crystal at something.

There were, of course, no surprises in the beginner swimming lessons the next summer, so I did much better, and I even jumped into the deep end. The instructors were so pleased that they wanted me to skip up to the advanced level the following year to be with my sister, which sounded like a good idea to my mom and me. I looked forward to making up for the time I had lost and, admittedly, the chance to be on the same plane as my sister again.

But by the next spring, we had moved out-of-state to a place where there wasn't a free community pool or low-cost lessons, so I never realized this particular dream. I felt shortchanged at the time, but now I wonder if it was God's way of reminding me that it was my job to be the oldest and that while I had to work hard to be the best oldest sibling I could be, being the best at everything didn't automatically come with the territory.

At some point in my early childhood, I began to notice how easy it was for Crystal to forgive people who had wronged her. I can remember telling her that I was sorry for something and feeling surprised when she smiled and said, "It's OK," and gave me a big bear hug. It seemed that her excitement for an excuse to give me a big, happy hug was greater than the personal injury she sustained from whatever I had done. While I stood with my arms pinned down by her enthusiasm, wondering how this could be happening, I also wondered whether it would be better if I responded similarly when other people hurt or offended me.

Perhaps her ability to take offense was somehow broken. For example, if my brother hit me with the head of my own doll, I would be incredibly upset with him for touching my doll, using my doll violently, hurting my poor doll's head, breaking the "no hitting" rule, and daring to hurt me. The actual physical pain resulting from that exchange was really an uncomfortable side consideration.

Maybe for Crystal, it was all water under the bridge once the pain had subsided because the other facets of the offense didn't upset her in the first place. Another possibility I considered was that she loved hugging us enough that this alone was sufficient motivation to forgive, especially since we were then less likely to squirm out of her grasp.

As she got older, I watched her and tried to piece together the mystery, but it seemed as soon as I got a couple more puzzle pieces hooked together, the puzzle would grow even larger.

We lived a mere fifteen-minute drive away from my paternal grandparents' farm for all of my childhood and adolescent years, and we visited the farm at least once a week. On that day, which was usually a Sunday or a Monday, we would pile into the family van right after dinner with Grandma Taylor and ride into the country.

These rides were magical and full of excitement and anticipation since there was nowhere any of us kids would rather be than Grandma and Grandpa's farm. I still remember the thrill I experienced every time our van would suddenly dip down from the road and onto the crunchy, crackly dirt lane that led to their house. I still feel that way now even when I'm the one driving.

We children found many ways to keep ourselves occupied on the way to the farm, some of which were more acceptable to my parents, such as singing or talking, than others such as arguing or drawing on the foggy windows with our fingers.

I personally liked to sing songs. I was very proud of my singing voice because many important adults in my life had complimented it and encouraged me to make good use of my talent, so I sang with great confidence and maybe a little bit of arrogance. I also preferred to sing alone, so I would sometimes choose songs to sing that only I knew. Even so, I recognized that I wasn't the only person with the right or desire to sing in the party, so I didn't protest if someone chimed in and started to sing along.

Unless that someone was Crystal.

I didn't have anything against Crystal's participation or her singing voice. The problem was that she didn't sing with me, she sang against me. She would sing faster or slower than me, but if I tried to change my speed to match hers, she would change speeds again. And if I tried to drown her out, she would sing louder. Stopping in disgust and glaring at her across the backseat was futile—she just kept on singing as if nothing had changed. Talking to her about the reasons why this didn't work or trying to get her to tell me why she wasn't cooperating didn't help either.

My parents would eventually either tell her to stop copying me or tell us that neither of us could sing anymore, which left me folding my arms in a huff to stare out the window instead and mentally cursing them for punishing me for a mean choice my sister had made.

This was beyond irritating. She wasn't just copying me and being an annoying little sister. She was insulting the art of music, abusing the beauty of singing, and disparaging the cooperative nature of singing *with* another person! In my mind, each of these crimes was offensive on its own, but they were utterly inexcusable together.

Strangely, I didn't usually say much about it. Was it because the whole thing was so unfathomable to me that I was rendered speechless, or was it because of the tempering influence of Grandma Taylor, who had a zero tolerance for arguing?

I'm not sure, but I will venture to speculate that it was for the best.

Crystal eventually stopped trying to sing over, around, or through me. I don't know why she did it or why she stopped. Now it's just one of the lonelier pieces of the puzzle.

One of the first things I learned in kindergarten, along with the alphabet and songs like "Danny the Dinosaur" and "My Country, 'Tis of Thee," was the fact that I lived in a free country.

What does it mean to live in a free country?

It means we can do whatever we want.

That's what I was told. When I asked for further clarification, I learned a little more.

Aren't there laws and rules we need to follow?

Yes, and people go to jail for committing crimes; however, people in other countries aren't as free as we are, and we should be grateful.

That summed up the lesson I was taught. I remained confused, but I was able to fill in the blanks in my understanding with some mixture of previous experiences and faith. It seemed evident that I was expected to feel very happy about this new piece of information, but it did not change the fact that I still needed to obey my parents and teachers, eat my vegetables, go to school, wear dresses to church, and all of the other tolerable, but slightly annoying, things I was expected to do on a day-to-day basis.

The question of how we were free if we still had to follow rules remained unanswered, but I had faith that I would solve that mystery some other day. It seemed clear that the fact that I lived in a free country was meant to inspire pride, joy, and gratitude in my heart, but it did not change anything I had already known about my life.

When Crystal learned that she lived in a free country in kindergarten, she did not travel as far down that line of logic as I did.

Suddenly, her behavior at home changed. If I caught her doing something against the rules and called her out on it, she would snap, "It's a free country!" and continue on as if nothing had happened. She responded to any attempt to explain the concept further with uncharacteristically hostile resistance.

Over the next few days, she broadened the horizons of her rebellion to include things she hadn't done before. My resolve to redirect her turned to exasperation, and my side of the argument disintegrated until our exchange sounded something like this:

"Don't do that!"

"It's a free country!"

"Is not!"

"Is too!"

"Is not!"

"Is too!"

"MOM!!!"

I finally ran to Mom and told her my woeful tale. When I came to her with problems with my siblings, she would usually greet my complaints with the same counsel: to ignore the offending party until they got tired of pestering me because they mostly wanted my attention and would stop if I ignored them for long enough. I was never completely convinced that this solution would work, but I had come to expect it.

This time, it was different, and I was very surprised by Mom's response.

After verifying a couple of times that I would not get in trouble for doing so, I returned to the living room to try Mom's proposed strategy. It didn't take me long to find an opportunity.

"Hey, that's my doll! Give it back!"

"No! It's a free country!"

I walked over and got her Amy bear off her bed.

"Hey! Give that back!" she said.

"I don't have to. It's a free country," I said.

"No, it's not!"

"Then give me my doll."

"No!" she said, clutching my doll as if I had made a grab for it. "It's a free country!"

"Then I can keep your bear."

"It's not a free country!"

"Then give me my doll."

"It's a free country!"

By now I could see the wheels turning in her mind, and this exchange didn't continue on for long before she got the message. She reluctantly relinquished my doll, and her newfound and freshly dashed paradigm, in exchange for her teddy bear. I proudly marched off to report the result of my experiment to my mom, who smiled wearily and said she was glad. It was a hard-fought fight but it ended decisively—Crystal never tried that tactic again.

I've always had an odd way of tying my shoes.

I came home from school one day and asked my mom to show me how. She asked me, "Do you want me to show you the hard way or the easy way?"

I thought that was a very silly question to ask someone who had never tied her own shoes before, but I was very respectful when I answered, "The easy way."

The way she showed me was the double bunny ear granny knot way that I still use today. When I came to the point in my life when I realized I was possibly the only human being on the planet who still—or maybe ever—tied her shoes that way, I asked my mom to show me the other way. She was happy to, but it was too late by then. I never could figure it out, but my shoes still stayed tied.

At the time I learned to tie my shoes, Crystal still couldn't tie hers. My mom wisely decided to turn this disparity into an opportunity for service. She encouraged me to use my newly mastered skill to help Crystal tie her shoes until she could learn how herself, and I was happy to do so. I loved being helpful. So for months or years afterwards, Crystal would come to me if her shoes were untied, and I would happily stoop down and tie her shoe. She would thank me and put on her coat to go play outside, and life continued on.

My great-grandma Taylor was very impressed to see this. She would often watch us play in the yard from her enclosed porch upstairs, and she would tell me later how happy it made her to see me treat Crystal so kindly.

Grandma Taylor and her sister, Aunt Betty, who lived in a little house behind ours, went to garage sales regularly and got all kinds of pretty knick-knacks for a nickel or a dime. One time while she was out, Grandma bought this little statue of an older child helping a younger sister tie her shoes for me as a present. It was quite a surprise, especially since giving random presents was not something she did often. It's a simple thing, but I have always cherished it as a reminder of service, and its deeper meaning has grown and changed with me throughout my life.

∾ 3 ∾

My Little Snow White

I was partway through fifth grade when my life changed forever.

I was enjoying close friendships, a teacher who enthusiastically encouraged my budding talent as a poet, success in almost every academic area, and the respect of almost all my peers and teachers. The future was both bright and excitingly unknown.

Then my father came home one night and announced that his company was closing and moving all of its operations to Mexico. He had been one of the employees who would be allowed the option of moving with the company while many others had simply been laid off. We had to seriously consider that option and make a decision soon.

Of course, it wasn't difficult to discern whether we *wanted* to go and leave the only home we'd ever known and family we could always count on for a far off and dried out desert land with only strangers to greet us. But that wasn't the question. The question was whether we *should*.

All of our family prayed and fasted and talked and cried until my parents ultimately decided to make the move. The company was paying for our move, so we would put all of our things in a moving truck and take six days to drive from our home in New York to our new house in Texas. I was terribly sad to leave, but I trusted my parents and decided to be a trooper, so I didn't cry.

On my last day of school, my class threw me a surprise going-away party and gave me a special book that they had all signed, which I still treasure. I collected my best friends' addresses and promised to write. When I got home from school that day, there were men in my house packing up everything that we didn't have to sleep on or eat over the weekend into boxes. I told them to be careful with my things. They told me they would be.

That Sunday was Elizabeth's eighth birthday, and the whole family and many of our friends gathered at the church for her baptism. It was hard work to not be sad on her special day, but there was great comfort in having everyone together for such a happy occasion. The next morning, as the sun was just barely starting to peek over the horizon, we seven buckled into our full-sized van and began our grand adventure.

It took six days to get there or, rather, we took six days. We could have flown—the company was paying for it—but my dad said he wanted it to take a long time so that we would understand that we couldn't just go back home if we got tired of Texas or go visit for a long weekend. He also wanted to make the trip fun, so we ate out at least once a day and stopped at interesting places along the way. We made some fun family memories on that trip.

At last, on Saturday afternoon, we arrived at a cul-de-sac and pulled into the driveway of one of the biggest houses I had ever been in. I felt a little spoiled, lying on my back on the carpet in the living room with my siblings, intrigued with how the living room shared its ceiling with the second floor, while we waited for the air conditioning to kick in. This place was huge—and beautiful! Maybe living in Texas wouldn't be so bad after all.

Once our things arrived, it was easier to believe that this was not a dream—I wasn't going to wake up one morning on the top bunk in the same apartment I'd lived in all my life. I had really left, and we really weren't going back.

There was only about a month or two left of school but, though I tried my best to convince my parents otherwise, we still had to go. My fifth grade class was held outside in a "mobile." It was a bilingual and integrated classroom, so many of my classmates spoke only a little more English than I spoke Spanish.

I had chosen my best-looking outfit for my first day, but several of my new classmates teased me for wearing long sleeves on such a hot day. There was a Spanish test that day, and I protested that I hadn't learned any of what would be tested, but my teacher told me I had to take it anyway. We graded our neighbor's test, and I was mortified to see 30 percent written at the top— the first failing grade of my life.

I struggled to pull myself together until my teacher asked for the grades. She called out the name of each student and made us each answer with our test grade so she could write them down in the grade book. I couldn't believe she would actually record my grade until she did it, and I lost it. I knew then that I had entered a world where life wasn't fair. That's when I cried.

As the hot days and weeks of school wore on, I lived for my art and music classes, which were both taught by the same teacher, as they offered a welcome break from my endlessly awkward school days. Mrs. Grey told me I couldn't join the choir this late in the school year, but she asked me to sing the solo part of a musical number that the whole class would be singing for the Earth Day celebration. I was so excited, and my parents were so proud!

On the day of the performance, I discovered that, for the sake of fairness, I would be sharing the limelight with a fourth grader. We never practiced together, and it wasn't awesome, but there you go.

I made a few friends during that short time, most of whom I lost as soon as we all moved to the bigger pond called middle school.

Please know that the names of all children in this book who are not directly related to me are fictional names. So, if you know an Alyssa Irie, rest assured that we're not thinking of the same person. I gave Alyssa a first and last name here because Crystal always used both.

The Irie family lived in the house across from ours in the cul-de-sac. There were three children, two boys and a girl. The boys were both a little rough around the edges but agreeable enough most of the time. We would play outside with them every once in a while.

Alyssa was not agreeable. She was mean and sneaky. She would speak to us sweetly and then whisper things to Crystal that neither of them would repeat if you asked them to.

You guessed it: Alyssa was Crystal's new best friend.

In a lot of ways, Crystal's relationship with Alyssa Irie was a rerun of her relationship with Corrinne, with a few notable exceptions. One positive was that Alyssa was a bit less bent on having Crystal completely to herself than Corrinne had been, or at least less aggressive about enforcing that preference. She was also a little bit more grown up, so their interactions seemed less childish.

Other differences were less positive. For example, Alyssa Irie would set Crystal up to lie or even get in trouble for her, doing so more and more often over time because it proved so consistently effective. She would also make Crystal do things that Crystal could see were clearly wrong before she did them, and Crystal felt bad enough to confess to Mom after she had done them.

I remember at least one time when my non-confrontational mother walked Crystal over to Alyssa's house to talk to her parents about what the two of them had done that day. Nevertheless, no matter how many times we sang the same "this is not how a friend treats a friend" refrain, Crystal remained loyal to her "best friend."

This emerging trend of finding bullies to befriend and be controlled by was naturally concerning to all of us, and by now, "all" included both parents and all four siblings. Even three-year-old Jessica protested when Alyssa Irie came over for anything.

We each did our best to steer Crystal away from this bully and toward better friends. Mom and Dad parented and prayed, I warned and bossed, Liz counseled and cajoled, Mark teased and poked, and Jessica fussed and whined. Nothing changed. Even in moments when she wished she didn't have to do such mean things in order to stay in Alyssa's good graces, Crystal never considered finding another best friend as a viable option.

So, our relief and rejoicings over having left Corrinne behind were disappointingly short-lived, and we all suffered—no one less than Crystal herself—for another three years.

We all had a lot of learning and adjusting to do in our new environment. We learned what to do if you got caught outside in a sandstorm and how to tip a water jug into the cooler. We adjusted to life in the big city, where Latinos were the majority. We also learned that Crystal's disability had a name and that we needed to adjust our expectations for her behavior.

Just before we moved to Texas, Mom and Dad had Crystal assessed for her disability and were finally given a diagnosis: Asperger's syndrome; however, since they already had enough bad experiences with this doctor to feel that they couldn't trust him completely, especially since the diagnosis was so huge and so outside of their experience, they decided not to tell us about it right away. They planned to seek a second opinion when they got to Texas. Without telling the new pediatrician what they had already been told, they had Crystal assessed again, and the diagnosis was the same.

This time, they believed it and told us what they had learned. The doctors had told them that Asperger's syndrome was "a mild form of autism." This syndrome was also characterized by delays in the development of social and problem-solving skills as well as lower physical strength, endurance, and stamina. People with Asperger's often did worse in some school subjects than their peers and better in others. My favorite piece of news was that many of the troublesome symptoms could be "learned out of," a piece of information I clung to for a long time. I guess, in some ways, I still do.

That's when we got all the books.

I remember looking through one of the books, *Asperger's Syndrome: A Guide for Parents and Professionals* by Tony Attwood, and reading the points of a checklist that was meant to help determine whether or not someone showed enough symptoms of the syndrome to diagnose them. I was concerned because, while I could see clearly that Crystal showed many of the qualities on the list, I could identify myself as having others. When I asked my mom about this, she reassured me that she and everyone else in the family had some of the symptoms on the list too and that having some symptoms didn't mean we had the same disability. A "syndrome" is a set of symptoms, and each symptom may be something anyone could have. This set my mind at ease considerably.

Unfortunately, that did not help Grandma-at-the-Farm, who saw so many of her own attributes in the checklist that she had to stop reading to keep from being totally overwhelmed. While it was uncomfortable for her, it shed some light on where this "difficulty" came from, so to speak, especially since she saw the attributes of her own mother, Grandma Taylor, in the checklist as well.

My uncle Steve, his wife, and his two small children came and visited us in Texas around the time Crystal was diagnosed, and they were welcome guests in our lonely world. I loved playing with baby Spencer. He had a cute little habit of quickly scrunching and releasing his hands into and out of fists with a huge gleeful smile on his nine-month-old face. His mother called it "crab hands" and figured it was just something some babies did and some didn't. We loved to play with the children and drew a great deal of comfort from their familiar presence in our strange new house.

I was also grateful to Steve for putting words to my feelings about living there. When he had moved into his first house away from The Farm a few years earlier, he had told Grandma, "This is where I live, but it is not my home."

He reminded me of this while he was visiting, and I was relieved to finally have words to describe my feelings. It was exactly how I felt about my new place in the world.

When Spencer was almost three years old, he was diagnosed with autism. For me, this added extra weight to Crystal's diagnosis. My parents already had all of their children, and they had a decent idea of the challenges they might face with each one. I, on the other hand, had all of my children to look forward to. Learning that four of my living family members likely had some form of autism made the prospect of raising my own children significantly more ominous than it had been when I rocked my baby dolls to sleep and played house with Barbies as a little girl. I have kept my mind and heart open to any information I could learn about the role of heredity in autism ever since.

Another adjustment for me was learning to deal with Crystal being better at something than I was.

During my few months of fifth grade, I was told that I could not join the choir for less than a school year. This was sad for me. My school in New York hadn't had a choir, and this choir allowed students to leave class for rehearsals, which I admit was a large part of why I wanted to participate.

I joined the choir in middle school, and Crystal joined the choir at the elementary school. She also joined Folklorico, a Mexican folk dance group—something I didn't even know was available while I was there, and for which there was no equivalent at the middle school. The only dance team at my school used immodest uniforms, and it was basically a jazzy cheer team anyway, so it wasn't at all appealing to me. Or it wouldn't have been if Crystal hadn't been taking dance.

I was jealous.

I complained to my mother and of course found no sympathy there, but she did help me understand myself and come to terms with what I was feeling. She explained that she was very happy for Crystal because Crystal had always loved dancing and really seemed to be doing well with Folklorico. Her teachers were good with her, and she was picking it up easily. She encouraged me to be happy for Crystal too and to be glad she had the opportunity to do something special that she enjoyed and could excel at. I said I would try, and I did.

It was hard, though. As the school year progressed, the excitement grew, and all kinds of bright and intriguing things started to enter our lives. First, Crystal brought home her bright, flowing practice skirt and special clogging shoes. Then one day, she stayed a little later than usual for practice because everyone was being measured for costumes. Another day, she came home to say that the costumes had come in and that she was disappointed that the color chosen for hers was blue because she wished it was pink. This was especially challenging for me because if I had the opportunity, I would have chosen blue for myself.

As Crystal became more and more familiar with the songs and dances, she would talk about the different parts she liked and didn't like about them and would hum the songs to herself around the house. All the while, I fought my feelings of jealousy and tried to be supportive and happy for her.

At last, the day of her performance arrived. Mom went early so that she could help Crystal get ready. When Dad brought us over, I was amazed to see how much was done to make sure this elementary school dance performance was a masterpiece. Every girl was wearing blush and lipstick, each had a costume that fit them perfectly, and each wore their hair up tightly with braids made of yarn and ribbons pinned around their ears in a Princess Leia hairstyle. I learned that heritage celebrations were serious business for the Mexican people.

When Crystal was ready at last, she came out to see us, and all of my negative feelings melted away in an instant. She looked amazing! She was truly the fairest of them all. Her makeup made her look much older, like she was a professional dancer in her twenties. The blue of the Folklorico dress brought out the best of her features in all of their glory, and she was the only girl whose hair extensions matched her actual hair color perfectly.

As I picked my jaw up off the floor, I realized all of my jealousy was gone. In my tomboy world of cargo pants and loose-fitting shirts, ponytails, and trying to stand up for myself without becoming a target for bullying, I would have been very uncomfortable on that stage. The makeup would have made me feel like a clown, the tight buns would have hurt my head, and the feminine, perfectly fitted dress would have made me feel like a doll on display.

Not Crystal.

She was fully within her element and radiant. I watched the polished and delightful performance that followed with a smile in my heart. I no longer envied her. I was *so* proud of her!

It was a time for growing into some things and growing out of others.

With Crystal's age now in the double digits and with her entry into middle school in the big city just around the corner, my parents tried to curb Crystal's thumb-sucking habit with renewed vigor.

Tabasco sauce stung her chapped skin and washed off too easily.

The solution in the magic little glass bottle of nail polish stuff tasted awful enough to deter her at first, but it wasn't waterproof. Enough of it would come off in the water when it was her turn to do dishes and irritate her skin painfully enough that she couldn't continue washing. And no, no one was willing to trade with her for chores that week!

And of course, explaining, lecturing, scolding, and gently reminding worked about as well as they ever had.

A few months after I turned twelve, I went to my first Girl's Camp, a four- or five-day spiritual outdoors experience that our church put together each summer for young women. Every year, I came back with a few souvenirs, a slight sunburn, lots of great pictures, and many wonderful memories. I always learned a lot about God, myself, and what it meant to love someone during that short time away from home.

I think it was partly because of this spiritual boost that I finally thought to turn to God for help on how to get Crystal to break her unsightly addiction in time to begin middle school. As I pondered and prayed for His help, I thought of a little key chain I had won at Girl's Camp. I then prepared what I would share with Crystal and what I would invite her to do with this unlikely tool.

Crystal and I shared a room in Texas, so it was easy enough to get her alone to talk. I remember the summer sun shining cheerfully through our window, and I felt encouraged that her face looked like she was really thinking about what I was saying throughout the exchange. I opened my scriptures, opened my heart, and then opened my mouth. I felt the Spirit of the Lord guide my words. I don't remember details, but I know I was enabled to communicate difficult concepts gently instead of using my usual lecture voice.

I told her she was beautiful, but thumb sucking was not a beautiful thing to do. Her fellow students in middle school would also not be as understanding of her habit as they had been in elementary school, and she would be picked on for acting like a baby. I read a couple of scriptures to try to encourage her to work on changing her ways with her faith in God, and I shared with her my feeling that God loved her and would help her change if she was willing to try. The look in her eyes was actually thoughtful and not disconnected or aggravated or obstinate. She said she was willing to try, which was a milestone in and of itself.

Then I pulled out the secret weapon I had felt inspired to offer her: the chunky, pink, clear, plastic dice key chain I had won at Girl's Camp. I showed her how it would work as I explained to her, "This clamp-style key chain is the perfect size to lock around the base of your thumb and stay there without hurting you. It's pink, your favorite color, so it can remind you to be happy. It is also bright with a little chain hanging from the clamp part, so even if you put your thumb in your mouth without thinking, you're unlikely to miss it. If you're really fast, it might even swing up and hit your face, and then you'll remember for sure. Then, when you can remember on your own, you can take it off and keep it because I am giving it to you. I know you can do this, and I believe you will be successful if you stick with it. Will you do it?"

She said she would.

She wore it the rest of that day, but not at all the next. She still twirled her hair for a little while longer, but she never sucked her thumb again. Now, what do you think of that?

As we both grew up little by little, I discovered to my surprise that Crystal and I actually had some things in common.

One of my favorite classes in school was Spanish. I loved how much sense Spanish made—I could read anything, even words I had never seen before, just because I knew the alphabet! Crystal loved languages too, so with Mom's encouragement, I decided to teach Crystal Spanish.

Not a stranger to the game of make-believe, I had no problem taking on the role of teacher by teaching vocabulary and giving and grading tests. I even typed them up on the computer so they looked official and were easier to read.

I know this sounds like the recipe for disaster, but I was growing up and learning to treat my little sister better. It didn't hurt that she was an attentive, enthusiastic, and patient student. She enjoyed our lessons too, though she didn't enjoy the tests as much as I did. I didn't try to trip her up because I wanted her to be successful. Sometimes, I even gave her little prizes when she did a good job, which she generally did.

I wonder if those lessons helped me more than they helped her because I reviewed my own vocabulary lists to make lists for her, but maybe that's not the important question. I think it's more important that we interacted together in a way that was meaningful to both of us, particularly since I was actively involved in doing some service for her. It helped me put her first, and it helped me learn about her in ways I may not have been able to otherwise. We had a good time, and we may have learned a little about Spanish along the way too.

I was a totally different person at home, though. With my family and good friends, I felt happy, confident, talented, and smart. I sometimes wondered how my family would react if they saw how different I was in school.

I have met a few people who actually enjoyed their middle school years, but most of the people I've associated with over the years agreed that middle school is best survived and then promptly forgotten. It is a time of intense competition, and your peers are judging your performance, whether you are interested in competing or not. And while the standard, I think, should probably be excellence, it is actually compliance in middle school. If you wanted to win, you needed to get as close to the arbitrary "normal" as possible.

I decided early on that normal was an inherently impossible goal to achieve, so I refused to compete. I embraced my place in the middle school world as the loner and weirdo, and I just went with it, only defending myself when necessary. My goal was not to compete, but to disappear, the idea being that the less the antagonists saw me, the fewer opportunities they had to make my life difficult.

Enter Crystal, stage left.

Her curly hair was bushy because she was trying to grow it out, and it always looked unbrushed no matter how recently she had brushed it. She wore oversized shirts and high-water pants sometimes. She joined in when the people in the movie she was watching started applauding. She laughed too loud and for too long when things were funny, especially when a cute boy told the joke. And, worst of all, she could be convinced very easily to bare her soul to anyone who smiled sweetly and promised to keep her secret. Every girl in her class knew who she liked this week and why. I felt like she was interfering with my cherished invisibility by being so unapologetically visible herself.

And yet, she didn't care. She was untouchable.

She didn't notice when people stared. It didn't hurt her feelings when people giggled or whispered to each other about her where she could hear. She didn't assume that anyone meant to hurt her with sarcastic comments or by spreading rumors. She didn't react even to direct teasing. She knew they weren't being nice, but it didn't hurt her. It was almost like a game she was learning to play as she went along, but she never got the memo that she was losing. That frustrated the people around her because a person who doesn't think she's losing in the world of social acceptance isn't actually losing.

I almost envied her, but ultimately, I decided to admire her instead.

I began to see that some of her "weaknesses" were strengths in this hostile place and that maybe there was something there for me to learn. Thinking of her this way made me happy, and it helped me think that maybe I didn't need to feel quite so picked on either.

I wrote a poem about Crystal, and while it didn't make the district-wide anthology like another poem had the year before, it did make it into the middle school anthology. That's probably where it fit best anyway. It was called "My Little Snow White" because seeing her dressed in her beautiful Folklorico costume made me think of that dark-haired fairytale princess.

As I read and re-read that poem, I realized that I had changed. I had made a choice to embrace her beauty, her talent, and her strengths. I was growing up.

Unfortunately, this internal maturation wasn't obvious to everyone.

After the school shooting at Columbine, every school across the nation scrambled into action. As the sometimes conflicting news and rumors of how and why it happened flooded our minds and homes, the question *How can we keep this from happening here?* rang in every school bell and PTA meeting, ricocheting off the walls of halls and classrooms, desperate to be resolved. We had extra fire drills and even a bomb threat drill, but my school's longest-lasting response was to tear out a huge section of lockers, thus compelling us all to carry everything we needed in backpacks.

It all seemed very futile to me. We students whispered to each other, not wanting to be overheard by anyone who might think we were actually planning something,

If I wanted to shoot people, wouldn't it be easier to conceal a weapon in my backpack than my locker?

Crystal got to use a locker in the special education room for her things. Since we got big gym lockers as eighth graders, a few of my friends and I stuffed what we could into them. With all of the exceptions and obvious loopholes, it started to seem like the school cared more about making sure everyone knew they were doing something than they cared about really protecting the students.

One of the effects of the shooting that bothered me the most was the prevailing rumor that the shooters were quiet kids who were bullied and oppressed and who never showed any signs of dissatisfaction with their universe until they finally snapped and took the whole world by surprise. It turned out this wasn't completely true, but it was a compelling story, and whenever anyone said, "I guess you have to watch out for the quiet ones," I could feel the pressure of nervous stares on the back of my head. So it was no surprise when I was one of the teacher-selected students to attend an all-day class, which turned out to be on anger management.

On the outside, I laughed with the two of my friends who shared my fate, guessing why we had been chosen for this experience, exulting about getting out of class for an entire school day, and challenging each other to a pizza-eating contest at lunch time. But inside, I felt sad that whoever submitted my name knew so little about me that they could worry I might have enough angst pent up inside to shoot up the school one day. I bet I wasn't the only one there who felt that way.

I told my mother at the end of the day about eating more pizza than all the boys at the all-day anger management workshop I was asked to attend. I was smiling as I told her about my day, and she smiled a little too, but her eyes were sad. I could tell she could hear the message I didn't have words to express. The look on her face perfectly reflected the feelings in my heart. I knew I was safe, I knew I was home, and I knew she understood. That was enough.

⌀

Another misconception I struggled with had to do with where people go after they die.

I believe that children need to be old enough to consciously make their own choices to understand the difference between right and wrong before they are baptized for the remission of sins as a condition of admittance into Heaven. In my faith, the "age of accountability" is officially eight years old. So in my world, babies are blessed, and eight-year-olds and converts are baptized.

With that understood, I eventually came to understand that in some cases, an individual might not reach their own age of accountability during their mortal life. Naturally, I believe that this is true of children under the age of eight, who we understand are saved through the overarching grace of Christ's atoning sacrifice and who are welcomed into Heaven to be with the God who gave them life. It makes sense to my mind and heart that a fair God, who called for the little children to surround him so He could be with them and bless them, would run His kingdom in this way.

Somewhere along the way, someone told me that people with disabilities were also saved automatically. Perhaps they were extra strong in spirit before they were sent to their earthly bodies, so they already had proven their conversion before they even got here, so they were given extra challenges in order to test those around them.

Whoever expressed this to me did so as if it were official doctrine and sound logic, but I never bought it completely. I could think of people with disabilities for whom this might be true, but the source was not official, and I wasn't ready to chime in with the chorus, a chorus which grew in strength and numbers over time, without thinking it through. I especially wasn't willing to entertain the idea—trying to was almost physically repulsive—that Crystal, with her "tiny" disability, would be just as off the hook for proving her allegiance to God as a young man who never mentally passed through all the stages of infancy. The mere possibility that this idea could exist in someone's mind seemed an injustice to her, to him, and to me.

Still, I struggled to find the truth for many years to come.

∞ 4 ∞

Dancing with Boys

The day we moved away from New York was the day Grandma-at-the-Farm started looking for jobs in the newspaper for my dad that would allow us to move back home again. She found jobs close to home from time to time, but nothing worked out for a long while. Finally, after three years in Texas, my dad applied for a job at a company similar to the one he was working for in Texas, and it was only half an hour's drive from The Farm. He was offered the job and accepted.

I can't speak for everyone in my family, but I was so excited to be going home that it was difficult to feel sad. We all agreed that our place in Texas was our house, but it wasn't our home. I had made some really good friends, and I was old enough to use the phone and Internet to communicate with people, so I was confident I could keep in touch with the best of my friends even from far away. I was also young enough to think that once I turned sixteen and got my license, I could take a road trip and come visit by myself.

I dreamed of being reunited with my best friends from elementary school and moving into a house right next to The Farm. This had also been a longtime dream of my parents, who had already bought the adjacent hay-field. I couldn't think of a greater blessing from God or a greater reward for the sacrifice we'd made by moving to Texas when we were asked to do so. I hoped I had done the work I was sent there to do, and I also hoped that the people I had touched—some of whom I was unaware of until they wrote in my yearbook—would remember me and that the positive influence would continue after I was gone.

Our family moved back to New York on my fourteenth birthday, and we were all happy to leave the desert behind us and live near our family again. We would be living in the old farmhouse with Grandma, Grandpa, and Uncle Dan while we waited for our house to be built next door. We were excited by the idea that we would begin the new school year attending the same school that Dad, Grandpa, and Great-Grandma Brayton attended in years past. We felt like we were continuing the Brayton legacy, and all was right in the world.

Moving into the farmhouse presented its own challenges. Uncle Dan was a senior in high school that year and was dating a girl seriously, so he was understandably concerned that his nieces would walk by and tattle on him. My mom, who had never had to live with her parents or in-laws in her fifteen years of marriage to my dad, struggled to deal with having a second mother in the house. But overall, we all enjoyed each other's company and had a great time being together.

Crystal began seventh grade on the same day I began ninth. All the children in our school district who went to school attended class in the same building, so Crystal, Elizabeth, and I passed each other in the hallways on a regular basis.

In any school, there's a certain level of hazing that every new kid must endure before they're accepted into (or assigned to) a group, and this school was no exception. There was a group of girls that welcomed me right away, and I enjoyed eating at their lunch table until the day they decided that I wasn't welcome there anymore. They never actually told me why, but I admit I enjoyed watching them fume when I refused to physically relocate until I had finished eating.

I understand forgiveness to be the journey required to root out the anger you feel toward a person who has wronged you and instead replace it with love. Ideally, when the journey is complete, you've grown closer to God and learned something about that person and about yourself in the process. Maybe that person didn't mean to hurt you, or maybe they did. Maybe you need to avoid certain places in the future, or maybe you need to work on becoming more difficult to offend. You learn from the journey, make a plan for the future, and continue on your way.

When the girls I befriended first decided they all hated me, I first defied them, then ignored them, then avoided them as it became clear that kicking me out wasn't sufficient punishment for whatever offense I had unknowingly committed. Finally, I had a spiritual experience while reading the Bible when it reminded me to "pray for those who despitefully use and persecute" me. Then I was able to bring my feelings to the Lord, and He helped me forgive and heal.

But it was different for Crystal.

I'm sure Crystal had some kind of journey too. Adjusting to life as the new kid in an unfamiliar school isn't an easy transition for anyone, but from my perspective, it was a much smoother process for her than it was for me.

Uncle Dan, who was a senior that year, and his friends had organized a not-so-secret service to protect Crystal from bullies. They even taped red arrows on the floor to help guide her from her locker to her classes until she could find them without help. She felt loved, and we were all grateful for their thoughtfulness, but this extra attention naturally made her a target for quieter forms of unkindness. Still, she maintained a sort of force field that kept hurtful remarks from touching her heart.

As I watched and listened in school and at home, I learned a few more things about Crystal's version of forgiveness:

Her best friends for many years were regularly unkind to her, but they were also sometimes nice to her. There were kids at church and school whom she avoided completely because they were only ever mean to her. So, I thought, she must be capable of differentiating between friends and bullies on some level. Maybe she automatically forgave people who were nice to her, even if it was only sometimes.

There was also a cute boy whom she gushed about at first, but after he persisted in being mean to her, she decided he wasn't so cute after all and stopped trying to talk to him. This seemed to prove that she was capable of learning to avoid someone whom she had previously wanted to like.

She couldn't help but bare her soul to anyone who smiled at her and asked about her life. This tendency could perhaps be traced to her difficulty with picking up social cues and knowing how to sense things like sincerity in people's facial expressions. But there were a few people whom she eventually learned to ignore completely because these people never meant to be kind to her and couldn't be trusted.

She often acted annoyed, frustrated, or embarrassed, but rarely hurt and almost never angry. Could she really forgive someone she was never angry with? Could she learn from a journey she never took? Could I get to the point where forgiving people was as quick and painless for me as it was for her, and if I did, would it be the same?

No, I don't think so. I've learned that while the Bible speaks many times about the importance of forgiveness, the imperative to "forgive and forget" is not scriptural. For Crystal, the goal seemed to be acquitting and forgetting what happened, while I strived to forgive and remember what I had learned.

As puzzling as this all was to me, it only took a few days for her peers to assign Crystal her fate. By the time the final bell rang on Friday, it was clear that she would fill two different roles at school until the day she graduated.

First, she became the go-to for a good laugh. She was so easy to annoy because she gave loud, dramatic reactions to teasing. She would answer any question you asked her, especially if it was followed by innocent eyes and a cajoling "I promise I won't tell anyone."

She came home every day with stories of her woes with this person or that one. If we weren't prepared to listen, or if she thought we wouldn't like how she handled a certain situation, she would retell the stories to herself in the bathroom instead. By week two at the new school, a few names became familiar, and I started paying more attention as I walked the same halls, trying to figure out who they were.

Looking back, I have realized that she didn't tell those stories of her run-ins with bullies the same way I would have told them. There was always a bit of a smile or even a laugh in her voice as she related them, and she always seemed to be at least a little disappointed when one of us interrupted her with a question or a solution.

Now I think she enjoyed the attention.

Her second and favorite role at school was as the "Special Ed kid." My parents, siblings, and I fought this classification, viewing it as beneath her. We were afraid she might use this label as an excuse to not try or not work as hard as she could.

But what could we do? She was welcomed, appreciated, taught, and understood in the Special Education room. Her peers were her friends and associates. Many of them had comparable abilities and struggles, and she was better than some of them at certain academic subjects. The majority of them were boys, and from time to time, two or three of them would compete for her attention. She even dated one of them for a year or two. Her teacher always had time and patience for her questions. Sometimes, fellow students even asked her for help with schoolwork or advice in relationships, and there was never a shortage of people or things to gossip about. It was the high school life that most of us could only wish for. It was real for Crystal, but it only existed within the four walls of the Special Education classroom.

After several weeks of wondering whether I would be doomed to four more years of "loner" status, I realized that I was simply sitting on the wrong side of the room during history class. Once I found my friends, I began sitting with them at lunch, and my whole world began to change. Over time, they became the at-school family I could only dream about in middle school. We learned about each other, tested each other, teased each other, and stood up for each other. It was a beautiful thing, and I know my mother was especially pleased that everything ultimately turned out so well for me in this new place.

Also during this time, I developed a relationship with God through prayer and scripture study, and I often recorded my experiences in my journal. I also found much-needed relief from the monotony that was being a gifted student in a mainstream school setting in books.

Crystal, on the other hand, would set a timer when she read her scriptures and stop reading as soon as it went off after the required daily ten minutes. She wrote essentially the same three sentences in her journal every night, and she prayed essentially the same prayer before she retired to bed. She read the *Babysitters' Club* and *Dear America* series almost exclusively at first before she later moved toward the YA fiction version of romance novels as she got a little older.

In my world, the scriptures I read helped me to understand and learn from the realities of life, and the books I read engaged my mind, taught me new things, and increased my vocabulary. In Crystal's world, scripture reading was a chore to be checked off along with washing dishes and vacuum duty. The books she read, on the other hand, served as an approachable version of reality that were incapable of teasing, judging, or scolding her. Books asked nothing of her. They were safe, and they were her friends.

She did have human friends as well. Her friends at church were my friends too. They loved who she was, and they patiently allowed her to hug them, which helped me in many cases to be more patient and accepting of her too.

School was a different story.

This time, thankfully, she did not find another bully to follow around like a puppy. Now, all her school friends also had special needs that were greater than hers in some or all areas. Of course, this was not a problem in and of itself; everyone needs friends, especially those with special needs that make them feel out of place. It was Crystal's attitude that became the problem. She acted as though she didn't need to work hard or improve because she was already as competent as or smarter than everyone she knew who mattered.

No matter how hard her family members tried to fight labeling and treat her like anyone else in the family, she lived like she *belonged* in Special Education. Other students tried to tease her about being "special," but it didn't bother her at all. She had already decided that the label suited her just fine, but I, for one, was not about to let her embrace her position as a less-than-capable member of society without a fight.

I remember one incident that occurred when we were talking as we crossed the street to go home. She was telling me about something dramatic that had happened to her that day, and I was giving her unsolicited advice on how she could have handled it differently, which was hardly an uncommon occurrence. When we made it to the front steps of our house, I asked her why she reacted the way that she had.

I can still see and hear her reply in my mind. She stopped, shrugged, threw her arms out, looked at me with her *duh, isn't it obvious?* face, and said, "Ashley, I'm Special Ed!"

In that moment, my stress about labels and their roles as excuses in her life, my concerns about her actual and apparent identity, and my worries about how long after high school I would have to continue helping to support her washed over me like ocean waves threatening to drown me. With all the energy and desperation of a struggling swimmer who finally made it to the surface for a gasp of air, I erupted.

"YOU ARE NOT SPECIAL ED!"

I can't describe the uncharacteristic volume I pronounced those words with. I'm sure no one in the house missed my part of that exchange.

All my anger left me with those words. I immediately felt ashamed of myself, and then all there was left to feel was sadness. I wanted to cry, and I thought maybe Crystal did too.

When I looked at her face, I thought I would find sadness or at least some penitence, and maybe even an apology, but there was none. Her once playful shrug dropped halfway, where it lay forgotten like a winter tree. Her face showed no sadness, only surprise—at first. Then a shadow came over her eyes that I didn't understand then, but I think I do now.

I believe what I saw was stubborn resolve. Not a resolve to do better, nor a determination to see herself as the wonderful individual she was rather than a member of a group of people with problems learning, but a resolve to never reveal her true feelings on that subject again. I unknowingly watched as she mentally added "I'm Special Ed" to the long list of things about her that her family members didn't want to hear about.

The thought that anyone, especially my own sister, would ever have need for such a list brings tears to my soul.

All of this transpired in only a second or two, as is true of many life-changing things. Trying to explain myself, I told her, "You are a daughter of God who loves you," and I recounted some of the things we had talked about in the young women's class at church that Sunday. Her face was courteous but uncommitted, as it usually was when she felt she was being lectured. When I finished, she said, "I know," and we went inside.

There was nothing left to say, but there was plenty left to puzzle about.

In that tiny school, I realized how likely it was that Crystal would have the same teachers in her mainstream classes that I had. I often wondered whether those teachers would have responded to her differently if they hadn't taught me first. My goal was always an A, and it was usually an easy goal for me to reach. I finished my work quickly and efficiently so that I would have time to read before class ended. I reviewed my notes before tests, and I did very well on those too.

Crystal was happy just to pass, and all of her quirky habits and her awkward aura followed her wherever she went. I wondered whether my teachers would be disappointed in her or expect too much from her, like her second grade teacher had, and treat her unkindly. It turned out that I had nothing to be worried about. She took alternative classes in many subjects because of her needs, and the few teachers we ended up sharing loved her for being so sweet and cheerful.

I still wondered about Mrs. Friday though.

Mrs. Friday wasn't around when my father was in high school, but she taught English to all of his younger siblings. She had a long-standing and fiercely maintained reputation for being the loudest, strictest, and least patient teacher in the school, if not the world. Many students, and even a few teachers, were afraid of her, and that fear seemed to be something she relished and even purposefully encouraged.

My brother wrote this poem about her when she was his teacher, included here in its original, unedited glory:

Friday the 13th
By Mark Brayton

'Twas a dark and rainy day,
Friday the 13th,
In dungeon #8.
Like a furious storm
A voice like thunder,
Sounded through the halls.
Friday the 13th,
The black eyes,
Like looking into the depths
Of an ancient library,
Alert to the education
Of these inmates,
Of this Hartford Central Jail.
Friday the 13th:
These black eyes
Stared into the faces
Of the juvenile division.
Her thunder boomed,
And her wind howled
And shook the foundation.

And the broom in the corner,

Fell with a clatter.

Friday the 13th-

As she stood in front of them

And she exclaimed,

In that all consuming voice,

The task

That these prisoners

Were deeply obligated to do,

Which included:

A five page report,

A hundred question test,

Annotate

Four acts of Shakespeare's Hamlet,

And write a practice Regents essay,

Just because.

All this due,

Friday the 13th.

> Dedicated to Mrs. Susan Friday,
> Esteemed English Teacher
> Friday 13th, April 2007

He actually gave it to her.

She *loved* it.

In this little high school with only two history teachers, two math teachers, and one teacher for each science class, there were four English teachers. With so many to choose from, students often chose to avoid her for as long as they could. Still, everyone knew that there was no escaping her because she was the only one of the four willing to teach drama, which was a required part of every senior's English curriculum. Sooner or later, every student would end up in Mrs. Friday's class.

Personally, I wasn't afraid of her. I refused to be afraid of her. As I endeavored to discover her motives, I realized that she focused her intimidation efforts on students who either weren't working hard enough to reach their personal academic potential or who were proud enough to act like they owned the school. In other words, she targeted slackers and those ill with "senioritis."

As I didn't fall in either category, I never had a problem with her. I actually tried to schedule her as my teacher for my first three years there, but it didn't work out. When I finally got to take her English class my senior year, I realized that what she really wanted for every student was the best they were personally capable of. She designed her curriculum around preparing us for college and the real world. All of her drill sergeant ways were just her way of making sure that anyone who stuck around this tiny town after high school did so out of choice, not because they didn't have a realistic enough view of the world or an advanced enough command of the English language to get out.

But what about Crystal?

She had always struggled with English, particularly composition, which was something Mrs. Friday really pushed for. Crystal also had challenges with fine motor skills, so she had never fully mastered handwriting or typing. After her years of taking English from a teacher who specialized in teaching students with special needs, how would Crystal do with Mrs. Friday in her senior year?

I had also wondered whether people would expect too much because, unlike many others in her classes, Crystal didn't *look* like she had a disability. Would Mrs. Friday be able to see Crystal's efforts for what they were, or would she put Crystal in the slacker category with the many others who had been satisfied with straight Cs before Mrs. Friday got a hold of them?

As it turned out, Mrs. Friday did more than understand Crystal. She became one of her most powerful advocates.

I asked my Mom about her impression of Mrs. Friday's class. She said,

"It was an IEP meeting where I met with all of Crystal's teachers that caused me to like Mrs. Friday. Since I'd heard so much that was negative about Mrs. Friday, I think it was more profound to me that she was outspoken in advocating for Crystal to stay in her class, even though Crystal couldn't do the work to the level where she would be able to take the Regents exam. Mrs. Friday wanted Crystal in her class, and she was willing to do whatever it took to help her pass it. I remember her saying how much she wanted her students to succeed and that when she got upset with them, it was because they did things that would keep them from succeeding. Right in front of my eyes, Mrs. Friday transformed from a temperamental meanie to a very caring and sincere person. As Crystal's mom, I *loved* teachers, students, and others who openly appreciated Crystal's gifts and potential and wanted to encourage and defend her."

Indeed, anyone in Crystal's class who showed her the slightest unkindness incurred the wrath of the dreaded Mrs. Friday.

I was also grateful to Mrs. Friday for seeing Crystal as she was and for treating her as a person with great potential. It helped me respect Crystal even more than I already did, and it also helped me think of ways I could do better in treating her that way.

Unfortunately, her peers were not as kind to her as her teachers were. By the time she officially began high school, it became painfully clear that while everyone around her was finally starting to get a handle on what relationships between boys and girls should look like, Crystal was only beginning to notice boys and develop feelings for them. As her classmates smoothly entered relationships and planned what they would do at whose house over the weekend, she was making all the blunders that the rest of us had left behind long before. The contrast was like red crayon on a white wall; it was impossible for even the most charitable passerby to ignore.

Thankfully, I was two grade levels ahead of her, so her mixed-up philosophy on how love should be, which she learned primarily from over-dramatic YA fiction, rarely affected me directly. Even when she decided she had a crush on the valedictorian of my class, who I had had my eye on for months, I didn't feel threatened. Mildly annoyed, yes, but there was no competition there. It was easy for anyone to see we weren't even playing the same game.

I will say that having her romantic daydreams flying around all the time did have some surprising side effects.

In my junior year of high school, my long-distance friend Matthew announced that he had saved up enough money from his part-time job to fly from England to our house for a couple of weeks if we would have him. He was considering attending an American university when the time came, and that was a just enough excuse. My parents talked it over and agreed that we could put him up in our home.

I was ecstatic. I was excited to meet my friend in person for the first time, but I was nervous too. I chatted with him online all the time, but I had only talked to him on the phone once before then, and his thick Yorkshire accent had made it almost impossible for me to understand him.

My parents prepared for Matthew's two-week stay by cleaning out a section of the basement next to the wall of food storage under the stairs and making it into a little bedroom, complete with its own door for absolute privacy. My parents' room was directly above it on the first floor, and my room was directly above that on the second floor. As a family, we planned out how we would fill our time during his visit, complete with bike rides, yard work, farm work, and the annual three-day youth conference the church in our area put on.

As Matthew came to visit my whole family, each of us got used to him and helped him integrate into the American family life in his or her own way. I ended up learning things about my friend through his interactions with my siblings that I wouldn't have been able to otherwise. In this way, Crystal ended up being instrumental in revealing some of his important characteristics, both good and bad, for me to consider.

One of these times was when a few of us kids were working with him outside in the sun. I remember feeling really good about how well I could chop at the dirt pile we would be using for soil in our garden. Yes, I was showing off, but only a little.

Somewhere along the way, Crystal said something silly, and Matthew teased her for it. It surprised Crystal, and I remember she looked really hurt and went into the house. It surprised the rest of us too, which I could tell surprised Matthew. We all turned on him, and his defense was that he teased his own siblings all the time, and he was just treating her like he would his own family.

My siblings and I were certainly guilty of being too judgmental of Crystal, giving too much advice too often, not praising her enough, and not giving her enough room to breathe, but we *never* made fun of her to the point of ridicule. We didn't take advantage of the way she said things to get a laugh or pretend something was true just to see her reaction. That just wasn't done in the Brayton house.

Actually hurting Crystal's feelings wasn't fun to do. She was so cheerful and so forgiving and so kind, and she had to deal with so much of the mean and miserable and unforgiving at school. Setting out to hurt her seemed like kicking a puppy. So we reamed him out like he had just kicked our puppy. I tried to be nice about it, but my mind was racing. *You are a guest in our home,* I thought, *and that is not how you treat your host family if you want to continue to be welcome. Besides, this isn't just any little sister. This is Crystal. Crystal is different, and treating her the same as anyone else isn't really fair.*

Of course, she forgave him immediately, and we eventually came to understand his perspective. No one held a grudge or brought it up again. But as I began to consider him as more than a friend, this experience kept coming back to me. When I remembered, I had to ask myself whether I wanted to spend my life with someone who teased his siblings so much that he thought that it was all right to tease other people's siblings too. I also wondered whether he would be able to handle being a kind, loving father to a child with a disability similar to Crystal's.

The following weekend, Matthew, Crystal, and I traveled down to the

annual regional youth conference put on by our church. One of my favorite parts of these conferences was always the dancing. I told my friend how
much I liked to dance, and he in turn gave me fair warning that he did *not*
like to dance. I was a little disappointed, but I tried to be understanding and
supportive while I got him to agree to at least come and enjoy the music.

Soon after the dance started on the first night, Crystal helped me learn
something else about my friend: Matthew didn't just dislike dancing. He was
afraid to dance.

I hoped Matthew would warm up to the idea of dancing, and I could
tell he was trying to psyche himself up to participate, so I tried to be a good
friend and talk to him between my favorite songs. If my other friends tried
to talk to him, I had to "translate" for him, even though they were technically
speaking the same language. When I slow danced with another guy, a friend
told me that he glared at us the whole time, and she and I laughed about it
together. I had to admit though that I was really falling for my friend from
England.

Once, when I wasn't looking, Crystal asked Matthew to dance, and he
said no. She got so upset that she cried and came to me to tell her sad tale. I
tried to comfort her and told her that he didn't like to dance at all and if he
wanted to dance with her, he would ask her. I asked her not to ask him again,
and she agreed.

After the next slow dance, I couldn't find Matthew anywhere. Finally,
when I looked outside the gym in the foyer, he looked back at me from one of
the couches, cowering like a frightened rabbit. Crystal had asked him again
to dance, and he had said no, which made her cry again, and it was so hard
for him that he'd decided to hide from her. He looked so sad and distressed
that I told him I would talk to her and then come back for him.

I hunted her down and grilled her about breaking her word. She was
defensive and upset, but I was unsympathetic at best.

I said, "He is in the foyer *hiding* from you because you asked him to
dance after you said that you wouldn't. You made him feel terrible when you

cried, and I don't know why you were surprised since we both told you that he wouldn't dance. How do you think that makes *him* feel? Now look me in the eye and promise you won't ask him again."

After several *but Ashleys!* and some dramatic sighs, she finally complied. I reported to Matthew, who cautiously returned to the gym.

"Fool me once, shame on you. Fool me twice, shame on me," as the saying goes.

After her first promise, I had been sure she would keep her word and leave Matthew alone. Now I had been reminded that I wasn't dealing with a younger Ashley, I was dealing with Crystal. So, as soon as I could identify the start of the next slow song, I whirled around and frantically scanned the gym for my sister. I was disappointed, though not entirely surprised, to find her headed—almost at a charge—toward Matthew.

I will never forget the look on her face. If steam engines had faces, I expect that would be the face they'd wear when they met strong storm winds. When I cut her off, she exploded with disappointment at being intercepted.

She was already explaining herself before I could even finish asking, "What are you doing?!" Her words jumbled and tripped over themselves, slipping on puddles of self-justified pity on the way down, and it started to sound like she hadn't convinced herself any better than she was convincing me that her actions were justified.

I put on my mommy face, reminded her that she was being dishonest and sneaky, and sent her away. She huffed off to find someone else to dance with, and I went over to Matthew, who had seen all but heard nothing, to report on my victory. He was relieved to hear the news and even more relieved when I sat by him and told him I would stick around. He was grateful for the company and I—well, it was hardly a sacrifice.

Only a few minutes later, it was my turn to be stopped in my tracks. I was so busy recovering from the adrenaline rush that had helped me catch and intercept a steam engine and scolding the DJ in my mind for playing a song at a dance that was neither a fast song nor a slow song that I couldn't understand what he said at first. I had to ask the poor kid to repeat it.

"Now that Crystal has left us alone, I can ask what I've been wanting to ask you all evening. May I have this dance?"

I must have said yes, but I couldn't hear anything over the white fireworks going off in my head. I couldn't talk or think straight. I could only stare at him, wide-eyed and swaying back and forth while I tried to put all the facts together. He had told me at breakfast time that he wasn't feeling well, and he hadn't eaten. As we were dancing, I learned that this was because of how nervous he was about asking me to dance that night. He had told Crystal no because he wanted me to be first.

He shared his first dance ever with me. Nothing could be wrong.

The next slow song was the last song of the evening: "My Heart Will Go On" by Celine Dion from *Titanic*. How perfectly cliché! But it *was* perfect. I sang it to him as we danced, and he smiled.

That night, I told my friends what happened, and they were more than happy for me. It was a high like nothing I had ever experienced, and my friends said they had never seen me happier. We sang Britney Spears songs in the car and did all kinds of silly things—our youth leader was more than accommodating and even joined in—until we reached the place where we would spend the night. I was the last to finish winding down and crawl into bed. As I reviewed the day's wonders one more time in my mind, I made a horrifying realization:

I couldn't remember the name of the song.

The song we danced to! The first one! The life-rewriting, unexpected beginning, starlit first song we ever danced to! What was the name of it?

It was no use. Everyone was asleep, and no one had any reason to remember it but me anyway. I tried to continue forcing my mind to give up the information, but I was so exhausted that my dilemma soon melted into a dream, and the urgent matter was thus compelled to wait until morning.

Everyone rushed around the next morning trying to get ready in time for breakfast. In the hustle and bustle, my question bounced around between other thoughts, surfacing for a moment and then disappearing again. Finally, as a last resort, I decided to ask Crystal what the song was; however, that day was so full of exciting activities and emotions that I couldn't get Crystal and my rational brain together at a good time to ask her until the whole conference was over and we were all home again. It was thus with little hope that I approached her with my question, but I reminded myself that if I never asked, I would never know.

"So, Crystal, I know this is crazy, but do you remember the name of the second-to-last slow song at the dance when I danced with Matthew?"

She reflected for half a second and then responded, "'I Don't Wanna Wait?'"

Of course! That's it! The slow song that wasn't really a slow song!

"Are you sure?"

"I think so."

"How do you remember these things?"

"I don't know."

And so it was. I don't know how she did it, but she remembered what I couldn't, thus enabling me to record every blessed detail of the conference in my journal to be preserved forever.

As I said, having Crystal's romantic daydreams flying around all the time had some surprising side effects.

That same summer, our entire family was blessed with the opportunity to participate in the Hill Cumorah Pageant. For us, this was only a four-hour drive from home, but many people had come from faraway states to spend four weeks as part of the pageant.

It was one of the largest outdoor productions in the world, but to us, it was more than that. It was a unique way to share our belief in Jesus Christ and testify by our participation that He was still important in our lives. Our experience brought us closer together as a family, increased each of our individual testimonies of the scriptures, and introduced us to many other excellent people who shared our faith and helped us strengthen it.

Audition day happened just a few days after we arrived. Because the script and musical score for the production was all pre-recorded, no one actually had to memorize lines. This took a lot of the pressure off, at least for me, and allowed me the courage to fantasize about the many different roles I would like to have.

Crystal and I decided to try out together for dancing parts. Auditions for some of the parts took place on the main stage, which was an enormous metal structure anchored to the side of the hill every summer just for this occasion; however, most of the auditions, including dancer auditions, were held on the great open field in front of the hill. The location alone was a natural test of our commitment to the parts we wanted because the auditions were held in direct sunlight in the middle of the day, sometimes for hours on end without a break. It was about all we could do to not give up and go home. Looking back, I know they were trying to be as kind as they could to all of us hopefuls—there were probably a hundred and fifty girls dancing around in the sun hoping to be chosen—but I still wish that they had just told Crystal and me that we didn't stand a chance. We saw people being pulled aside and sent elsewhere, but we weren't sure why at first. By the time we figured out that they were the ones moving on to the next level, we didn't want to quit in case we were about to be picked or in case everyone would get some good role just for hanging in there.

After they released us to our parents, Crystal and I hobbled back to camp. I was impressed that she had held out for so long because her stamina had always been a challenge for her, and my stamina had been challenged to the max that day. All either of us wanted was cold water and a nap.

Everyone made their way back to camp little by little to take a rest and get something to eat. By the end of the day, all of us had a role and knew what scenes we would be appearing in.

During the rest of our time there, we enjoyed the time we spent on our own with friends our own age. We practiced for our various scenes, and our experiences helped us think about the scriptures in personal new ways. But the time we spent together helped us to really think about our real life roles as members of a family.

There was one scene in the story where almost everyone in the over 750-person cast was on the stage at the same time. The organization of the actors in this scene was different from the others, as we weren't grouped by cast teams but by families. This was intentional and meant to help us better act out our parts; in this scene, the characters in the play got to meet the Savior face-to-face.

The directors who guided us during rehearsals wanted us to make this scene personal. They wanted us to try to forget that the "Jesus" we were waiting for was just a nice guy with a fake beard. They encouraged us to really think about what it would be like to see the Savior face-to-face and being able to share that experience with our families. For me, I found additional meaning when I remembered that Jesus promised that He would come again, so I might yet have the opportunity to do for myself what my character was doing almost two thousand years before.

What would that be like?

A spirit of reverence covered all of us on the stage as we practiced and performed this scene. The wordless awe was electric as we climbed the stairs up to our place on stage. My mom and dad held hands. They kept us together with a gentle touch on an arm or a grasp of a hand as the huge crowd around us moved to get a better view of what was happening. When we could see Jesus, my siblings would sometimes point toward Jesus to show each other where He was. During practice, the director said he would need about a third of us to kneel when Christ appeared, so my dad and I went down on one knee each night. There are no words to describe how it felt to see my dad in the way I picture him responding when he really meets the Savior someday and to share that moment of worship with him.

Off-stage, we were Mom, Dad, Ashley, Crystal, Elizabeth, Mark, and Jessica. We had different interests, aptitudes, personalities, and roles. But during this scene, we weren't even the Braytons. We were simply family. All of us watched and listened as a unit. We looked alternately between Jesus and each other, making sure none of us were missing any of it and that each one believed what he or she was seeing too.

The more I thought about what it would be like to really meet the Savior face-to-face, the clearer it became to me that I wanted every single member of my family to be with me when I did. I realized that no matter how difficult or annoying they might be at times, there was no doubt in my mind that everyone belonged there. No one should be missing. I wanted to always remember that feeling—the feeling of connection among my family members and the bond between our family and the Savior.

I pray that we will all be there to worship Him the way we did on that stage when He comes again: in reverent awe and together.

The production began every night at about sundown. There was open and free seating, and the guests would start saving seats hours before show time, the most committed of them arriving close to breakfast time. Starting about two hours before show time, the cast members would don their costumes and then go around in the audience welcoming people to the pageant. We would move within our designated areas in pairs or small groups and try to make sure everyone in the huge crowd talked to someone in the cast before we heard our cue to line up for the opening sequence.

I loved talking to people. Everyone had a story. Some people had questions about our church or the story we were telling while others wanted pictures or autographs, and everyone was happy to see us and glad to be there.

I didn't expect that my career choice would be influenced at all by this very faith-based experience, but I learned that God could give us direction anywhere as long as we're paying attention.

One night, a pair of my friends who had been welcoming people closer to the stage came up to my friend and me, looking a little embarrassed and a lot scared, to ask us for help. They said that there was a group of adults in their area with mental disabilities and asked us to come and talk to them. I was surprised by their fear, not because I judged them for it, but because it seemed like an easy thing to do to me. I told myself that it was probably easier for me because I had more practice, and I felt grateful for the chance to serve my friends and these adults.

The group was close to the front so they must have been there for a long time, but they were clearly enjoying themselves. Most of them were middle-aged men, and there were a couple of wheelchairs in the bunch. All showed evidence of their challenges in the shapes of their faces. I was a little nervous at first but not much more than I was every time I went to welcome someone new.

Everyone there seemed as happy as could be to be alive, and I was soon set at ease. Their caretakers were some of the most attractive, cheerful black women I have ever met with big hoop earrings and bigger smiles. The spirit of loving people, loving life, and loving God was all around them. Those they cared for were happy to receive matching welcome stickers to put on their matching shirts, and they were glad for the kind attention that we were giving them.

As we walked back toward our area, we met our relieved and grateful friends who thanked us for coming and helping them. It all got me thinking that maybe, if my skill set for talking to and helping people with disabilities was so uncommon, I should think about going into that line of work. Then I could be of service to these people whom apparently few others knew what to do with. Thinking about my future major in college was actually something I did often at seventeen.

My various ponderings over the course of that summer helped lead me to use some of my free time to volunteer in the Special Education classroom in my senior year. This decision really brought into Crystal's world and helped shape me and my life's path from that point forward. Many of the people I met as a volunteer influenced my view of people, disability, and the world.

Two of Crystals' classmates in the Special Education room were technically in my graduating class. I'll call one Loren and the other Gage.

Loren and Gage were good friends, even though their abilities varied widely. I honestly wouldn't have guessed that Gage even had a disability if I hadn't seen him in that class. He was quiet, but he looked you in the eyes when he talked to you, and his eyes showed evidence that he was an intelligent and thoughtful soul. I really liked the way he interacted with his kid brother. He acted like he cared for him and felt responsible for him. I think he had been able to keep most of his classes mainstream with just a little adaptation.

If Loren was essentially a two-year-old in a twenty-one-year-old's body, he was the sweetest two-year-old you could ever hope to meet. He could walk and smile and more or less make his will known, but he could only say a few words without having just heard someone else say them, and he had a teacher's assistant with him at all times. He made me nervous at first. I guess I didn't know whether he might spontaneously decide to lash out and hit someone. But as I got to interact more with him, it became easier to see past the surface noises and mannerisms to the kind person he really was.

Gage didn't seem to find it difficult to see Loren for who he was. He didn't act like Loren's defender or even like some kind of compassionate hero. He treated him like an equal and like a friend. He spoke to Loren with the same evenness and respect that he used with his teachers and everyone else. The teachers trusted Gage so much that they even occasionally sent him to accompany Loren on an errand in the place of the teacher's assistant. Gage was a great example for me of how people should treat others, no matter what "level" they operated on. He helped me rethink how I treated Crystal too.

There was one evening I wished Gage rode the same after-school bus.

Loren and his sister, who was probably in eighth grade, rode home with me once on the after-school bus. The two of them seemed to have a similar relationship to what I remembered having with Crystal when I was in middle school. Loren's sister was mature for her age, like adults had always told me I was, but she was also tired like my grandma could always tell that I was.

Some boys on the bus, who seemed to know her from class, got Loren to parrot them. Loren loved the game, and he laughed harder and harder as they went along. He didn't know what he was saying, he just knew that he was getting lots of attention and making people happy. The boys kept looking sideways at his sister and took her awkward laugh and failure to protest as permission to continue their game.

As the words they had Loren say got less and less appropriate, I got more and more uncomfortable. Loren just basked in the attention that he was getting from his smiling peers. I was disappointed that his sister didn't intervene, but I didn't know how or whether to step in myself. I told myself that it was her job. I didn't know her or Loren well enough to act responsible for Loren, and I wasn't the high man on the totem pole in this situation. I was afraid all the teasing energy on the bus would be turned on me if I spoke up and drew attention to myself by being disapproving of their actions. So I stayed quiet. They eventually ran out of new words, and Loren and his sister got off the bus.

I've always wondered what would have happened if I had stood up for Loren.

But God is good and gave me other chances to help Loren out.

When permission slips were due for my class's senior trip to Boston, I learned somehow that neither Loren nor Gage would be joining us. It seemed to me that their parents were nervous about them being away from home and surrounded by the influence of other vacationing teenagers with various maturity levels for the three days of the trip. I was sad that they couldn't come. I thought they would have fun with us, and I would have enjoyed spending time with them too.

On our first day in Boston, we watched the Red Sox play baseball at Fenway Park, and we visited the Boston Market for souvenirs before checking into our hotel for the night. Once most of my classmates had dispersed, Mrs. Friday called me and two other girls over to her. She gave us some money and told us to go to one of the shops that sold Red Sox baseball caps, buy two, and then go to the embroidery shop to get "Loren" embroidered on one and "Gage" on the other. She asked us not to tell the other students in a low gentle voice, which told me that we were about to be sent on a top-secret mission. She told us how to spell Loren's name, and we ended up writing it out on a little piece of paper so that we wouldn't forget it. I felt both honored to be chosen and grateful to be able to participate in the acquisition of such special gifts.

Months later, on a hot summer day, Crystal and I attended Loren's graduation party. I don't know why I was surprised to see so few people there. It was clearly an exclusive event and more like a special outdoor get-together than the big parties I had been to for my other friends.

Loren's mom showed us where the food was and thanked us for coming. Once we had sat down with her, she thanked us some more for coming and told us that she had only invited his teachers, Gage's family, and us to come. She also thanked me for helping to get Loren the Red Sox cap.

Mrs. Friday must have told her the whole story because I certainly had not broken my promise to keep quiet about it. Loren's mom was clearly touched, and I felt even more grateful that Mrs. Friday had involved me in that small but obviously well-received act of service for one of the brightest spirits with the greatest hearts of anyone I have ever met.

Crystal's best friend in high school was a boy that I'll rename CJ. He spent a lot of time with Crystal because they took many of the same mainstream and Special Education classes together. Crystal would also sometimes attend activities with him and his girlfriend, who went to another school, after school and on weekends. She always denied that she liked him, and she never tempted him to be unfaithful to his girlfriend in any degree.

During my first vacation home from college, my mom asked me if I would be willing to help chaperone Crystal's first school dance. I can still see her face in my mind with her expression that said, "I know I always ask you to do this kind of thing, but I really hope you won't be unhappy about it."

I was more than happy to accompany Crystal to the dance. Mom and I agreed that an after-school dance was hostile territory, and Crystal should have someone there to look out for her. We also agreed that it would be beyond uncool for her to have her mother there at the dance but less uncool for her sister to go. So I dressed in my best don't-mess-with-this outfit, fixed my hair to look as much like a teacher's as possible, and drove Crystal to the Winter Ball.

We were happy to see her friend CJ and his girlfriend there, and she didn't seem to have any problem with not having a date of her own to dance with. She enjoyed herself immensely, and CJ even asked her to dance for a couple of slow songs. I stood at the side and chatted with the principal, who seemed glad that I came. All went well for at least an hour, which was impressive because Cody Sparks was there. He was the most popular boy in the eleventh grade, and Crystal was Cody's favorite target.

Crystal loves to dance at least as much as I do. She has actually said many times that she would most like to be a famous singer or dancer someday. She had never taken lessons, but it was one of the things she could do that made her feel free. You could tell by the way she moved. Her whole soul danced with absolutely no concern for the people around her, beyond trying not to run into anyone.

Her dancing used to embarrass me until I realized that she might actually be the only one doing it right. After that, I danced next to her sometimes at the church dances that we attended together. It was my way of letting everyone know that I endorsed her behavior and welcomed them to join the fun too. But at the Winter Ball, I was obliged to act as an adult rather than as a peer. She was on her own, so it was only a matter of time before the teasing began.

I watched the first incident from a distance. Crystal was dancing in her usual way, unrestrained and alone, with a huge empty circle around her as if everyone else there was trying to avoid catching her disease of uncoolness.

Cody approached with a smirk and a swagger, accompanied by the silent attention of his many adoring fans. Crystal looked up, he spoke, she turned, tipped her head forward, and walked away with long, determined strides. Cody paused for a moment, probably imagining what he would say to his admirers when he returned empty-handed.

I couldn't have been more proud.

When I found her and asked her what happened, she said that he had asked to dance with her, and she had walked away without even answering because she knew his intentions were anything but kind. He had proven his true colors long before, and she had no problem seeing through his guise of friendliness to a joke at her expense waiting to happen. I told her how proud I was of her for not making a big stink, or worse, actually letting him dance with her. I was a little surprised and, of course, I was *very* pleased.

Not one to be robbed of his place in the limelight, Cody tried again. This time, Crystal could see where I was and headed straight for me.

He made the mistake of following her.

I can't remember what I said to him, but I know I opened my can of protective older sister and let him have it. There was a fair amount of "what pleasure do you get from picking on someone with a disability?" with quite a bit of "do you actually think that hurting people makes you a bigger person?" mixed in, I'm sure.

I also know I won. He tried so hard to save face, but at last, he wisely discerned that continuing on would only give his cronies more to laugh about once he finally retreated. I can't say that he walked away like a dog with his tail between his legs, but he did seem a notch or two humbler than he was at the start.

We didn't have anymore trouble the rest of the night.

By Crystal's junior year, CJ and his girlfriend had gotten tired of each other, and he decided that he wanted to date Crystal. This was great news for her. He also insisted on being called Charles instead of CJ, a change that Crystal enforced among her family members with an almost ridiculous level of enthusiasm. It was as if she felt she was defending the honor of her one true love every time she had to correct us. The gravity that she had hoped to convey was of course lost on us. We just joked with each other about his newly refined identity while Crystal listened, looking like she couldn't decide whether to laugh with us or try again to get us to stop teasing.

They spent time together like friends in grade school. They were almost continuously chaperoned, even on "dates" since neither of them had a driver's license. Still, the rest of us found it ironic, and too unfair to be funny, that the most socially awkward member of our family was the first to have an official boyfriend. *C'est la vie.*

They went to prom together, and Crystal dressed up in pink and had someone do her hair and makeup. She had a great time, and we were all glad that she could realize every girl's princess dream of going to prom with a date.

But soon after "Charles" graduated, he got tired of her too and broke off the relationship. He was kind about it, which we all appreciated, but she would hold onto that kindness for months as an indication that he might call back any day and say that he had changed his mind.

He never did. In fact, she hasn't heard anything from or about him since.

When the time came at last for her to think about graduation, it all boiled down to two options: get a modified special education diploma—which wouldn't be worth much more than the paper it was printed on—or try for her GED. Crystal decided that earning something she could actually use was worth the extra work, so she started preparing for the GED.

I was very proud of her for choosing that option. It still took some adjustment to think of it as positive though. In our family, everyone had graduated from high school, so thinking of Crystal getting her GED—one uncle said he used to joke about it with his friends and call it the "Good Enough Diploma"—was not a happy thought right away; however, by the time she took and passed it—on the first try!—we were all very pleased.

Mom had me take some money and go to a local floral shop to order Crystal a special bouquet. I was glad to be able to participate in the celebration this way. I really enjoyed thinking about what she would want in her bouquet and placing the order. *A few roses, she loves those. And some daisies, yes, they're so cheerful and so like her. Beyond that, be creative and make it bright and beautiful. And instead of a vase, put the flowers in this smiley face mug. Just seems more fitting.*

I was astounded at the end result. It was light, beautiful, cheerful, smiley, *perfect*. And she loved it. Mom and Dad took pictures of her with her GED diploma and her bouquet like they took pictures of me when I graduated from high school. After all, it was a huge milestone for her and a big deal for all of us.

I think we still have the bright smiley face mug because I've seen a very similar-looking mug at home in the same cupboard as the cereal bowls.

Mom, Crystal, and her teachers tossed around different ideas about whether Crystal would want to finish the school year or walk at graduation. After all, her classmates were hardly kind to her, and it might be a welcome break to leave them at last. She ultimately decided to keep going all the way to the finish line, and I was glad.

I was at school and couldn't come to the ceremony, but I really wanted to be there for her on her big day to help her celebrate. So I came up with a crazy idea and looked at my finances. When I called Dad to tell him about my idea (I was afraid Mom would be too excited to keep it a secret), he liked it and agreed to meet me partway to help me buy a plane ticket so I could be there for that weekend.

I didn't tell Mom until the last possible moment, and she was excited beyond words that I was coming. We planned it out perfectly: Mom would pick me up from the airport, and she and I would go together to pick Crystal up from her graduation practice that day.

Once we made it to the school, Mom went in to get Crystal, and I hid behind the Jeep to wait. At last, I heard them coming, and when it sounded like they were close enough, I jumped out of hiding.

"Surprise!"

"ASHLEY!"

Crystal ran to me and gave me a big squeeze. She was every bit as excited, dramatic, and gleeful as I had imagined she would be, and she carried on for a good while.

Graduation was the next day. I saw a few friends there who were also watching their siblings walk. It was a joyful occasion, despite the heat in the gym that could only be cooled by one huge fan set up by the outside door.

The last part of the evening's program was the traditional candle-lighting ceremony. Crystal lit Elizabeth's candle with her own candle before blowing her own out, just as I had lit hers and Uncle Dan had lit mine and all the way back as far as anyone could remember.

I wondered whether it meant anything different this time. The light that she was physically sharing was the same, but the symbolic light was different. What was she passing on to those who would follow her? How many had their candles ready to receive the light that she offered?

I hope someday we'll find that those questions have answers.

After all the celebrating and picture taking was over, Crystal found out what every high school graduate eventually learns: graduation is a milestone, not the end of the road.

∞ 5 ∞

The Challenges of Reality

After she graduated, Crystal was hired at the grocery store bakery where she had volunteered during high school as part of the work-study program. She had worked there for a while before money became tight and everyone's hours were cut. They reduced her hours from ten a week to one or two, if any. She didn't understand why they did it, and neither did we because she always cheerfully and patiently did what she was told.

Personally, I think that if they had a good reason, they would have let her go. It would have been illegal to fire her due to equal opportunity laws, so they invited her to leave on her own by cutting her hours.

At last, after weeks of searching for an explanation and having someone drive the forty minutes both ways to bring her to and from work, Crystal handed in her two weeks notice. It was the family's first encounter with what I now call relational violence firing.

After some time, and with some help from a job coach, she got a job wiping tables and keeping things tidy at a McDonald's. Problem solving became a huge issue for her there because she didn't want to ask for information such as where she could get something to drink, what to do on rainy days when there were fewer customers, and how long the lady she was picking up hours for would be out on leave.

Ultimately, it was fatigue that got her. She started with a short shift once a week and then moved on to working three days a week for long enough hours that she didn't think she could go on. She quit there and looked for something else. I asked later whether she ever asked the manager for fewer hours, and she admitted she had never thought of that as an option.

Her job coach helped her find another job, this time at the cafeteria of a Catholic school for girls. She loved this job. She loved her co-workers, and they loved her.

Because I understood that my parents would still have four children at home and could not help me much with my expenses, I had worked hard in high school to save up for my education. I also worked part-time in college and always tried to do my best because I knew the grades I earned could also earn me much-needed scholarships. I thought I had started out knowing who I was, and maybe I did, but my experiences in college—which was the first time I was really on my own—helped me refine my identity.

I had mentally measured and balanced everything I knew about myself and everything I felt the Lord wanted me to do when I considered what to choose for my major in college. I wanted to be able to teach in schools, but majoring in special education wouldn't certify me to teach in mainstream classrooms. I also didn't want to teach above a third grade level, but pre-school education seemed too narrow. Elementary education seemed the best of my available options.

My mother had warned me, in good humor, that when she went to school, people teased the girls who majored in elementary education, saying that they just wanted to learn about teaching children for long enough to catch a guy and graduate as soon as possible. I knew that wasn't true for me, and I was fine with being teased if someone wanted to do it. I did hope, though, that the stigma would have changed at least a little in the past twenty years. I also hoped that I could somehow take extra classes and earn a special education endorsement so that I could choose to teach in either elementary school or special education classrooms.

My decision to attend all the activities associated with freshman orientation before classes began was one of the best decisions I ever made. I made many new friends there, and it was through my associations with them that I learned the most about who I was by myself. But perhaps more importantly, I attended my department orientation, where I learned what I should choose as my major.

The first speaker at this orientation represented the elementary education major. He explained what the major covered and some of the classes that would be required. At the end of his remarks, he stated that there was no special education endorsement available for elementary education majors at that time. He sat down, and my mind started racing. *I guess I will have to get a master's in special education if I want to teach both. I wonder how many more years that would take?*

The next speaker was Joyce Anderson, who would soon become my personal hero for more reasons than one. She announced, with both excitement and anxiety in her voice, that beginning that semester, there would be a new education major available in early childhood/special education. This course of study would give students a blended certificate that could be utilized in careers serving children from birth to third grade, whether they had special needs or not.

This confirmed a couple of my long-held beliefs as being absolutely true. First, there is no such thing as coincidence. Second, there is a God in Heaven who loves me very much and who wants me to succeed.

I changed my major from elementary education to early childhood/special education (EC/SE) as soon as I could. I was determined to begin this new phase of my life with my eyes wide open and my arms outstretched.

One of my first classes was Foundations of EC/SE, where I was fascinated by the history of special education, special education laws, and the differences among the cognitive theories of great minds such as Jean Piaget. I ate it all up; I was so excited and grateful, though sometimes overwhelmed, to be learning so much about a topic I cared about.

One day, our class discussion brought up a disorder I had never heard of before that was called sensory integration disorder. It came up because my professor said that if we noticed a child rocking habitually in his or her chair, this was probably the cause.

My mind exploded. *I rocked as a child.*

I had rocked on the couch and in my bed, listening to the noises they made, and I was both comforted and fascinated to hear the same sound every time I hit the back of the couch with my body. I would imagine that the sounds were words, and I would try to decipher them. Then I would sing along to my rocking song.

Do I have sensory integration disorder?

I asked my professor after class whether a child who rocked might have something else instead.

She said, "Well, maybe Tourette's."

Whoa. I knew I didn't have Tourette's, so it had to be sensory integration disorder. As I walked to the library to do some homework, my mind brought me back to childhood, and I wondered what it all meant. By the time I got there, I couldn't do homework until I had learned more about sensory integration disorder.

I searched online, naturally.

Now the official name has changed to "sensory processing disorder." Here is a good definition from the SPD Foundation website:

> *Sensory Processing Disorder can affect people in only one sense— for example, just touch or just sight or just movement—or in multiple senses. One person with SPD may over-respond to sensation and find clothing, physical contact, light, sound, food, or other sensory input to be unbearable. Another might under-respond and show little or no reaction to stimulation, even pain or extreme hot and cold. In children whose sensory processing of messages from the muscles and joints is impaired, posture and motor skills can be affected. These are the "floppy babies"*

*who worry new parents and the kids who get called "klutz" and
"spaz" on the playground. Still other children exhibit an appetite
for sensation that is in perpetual overdrive. These kids often are
misdiagnosed—and inappropriately medicated—for ADHD.*

I also found a list of indicators of sensory integration disorder and could
hardly believe what I was reading. It was like reading Crystal's checklist years
ago, except this one was mine. Finds simple things like brushing hair or
trimming nails unreasonably painful. *Yes! I agonized and screamed for both.
Poor Mom.* Unusually poor handwriting. *Yes! And I thought it was because of
how I held my pencil!* Extreme response to loud or high-pitched noises. *Yes!
Sometimes embarrassingly extreme.* Poor posture. *Yes! I hope that can be helped.*

It was like I was finding myself. Who could have guessed that so many of
my quirks had the same cause?

Another surprise was that almost every item I answered no to, such as
"high tolerance for or indifference to pain" and "extreme fear of falling" would
be a yes for Crystal. This connection was one I would never have expected,
and it made me wonder if I also had some sort of autism as well. But the site
made it clear that while it was common for children with autism to have
sensory integration challenges, many who did have sensory integration
challenges were outside of the autism spectrum. So I came to the inevita-
ble, though very unexpected, conclusion that Crystal and I both had sensory
integration disorder, but we just experienced it in different ways.

I was so excited with my discovery that I immediately e-mailed my mom
to tell her what I had learned. Then I tried to pull my mind back down to
earth so I could work on homework. Still, I wondered whether I could find
someone to diagnose me this late in life. I wanted it to be official so I could
tell people what I had learned about myself and put a real name to it.

I was a little disappointed that my mom wasn't as excited as I was to
hear what I had learned, but that was easy enough to understand. She'd had
enough of labels and disabilities, and I imagined that she also needed me—
the OK one—to stay OK. I respected and understood where she was coming

from, but I decided I could be excited about it anyway, especially if I actually implemented some of the strategies I learned about so I could improve my life.

As I clicked and read and clicked and read some more, I couldn't tell which was more exciting: learning that there was an explanation for why I felt a certain way about things or learning coping strategies for managing some of the difficulties these "symptoms" still caused me.

That knowledge I gained in my first semester became more and more important to me as I got further along in my schooling and had to work harder and do more for the grades I earned, especially as late nights and early mornings became standard fare. It was a huge comfort to know what was going on, and what I could do to help myself feel better.

On our way to dropping me off at school for the first time, my dad and I had stopped at my aunt and uncle's house a few hours from the school. Their son Spencer was about six and had recently started an intensive therapy program aimed at helping him learn around his autism to communicate verbally. My memories of that visit gained new significance as I thought about it in the context of sensory integration in my immediate and extended family. I wrote a piece about my observations of Spencer and his family for an English assignment.

When I talked to Spencer's mother about it later, she said she had "sensory integration issues" too, and figured everybody does to one degree or another. That rang true to me, and it really made me think. Could it be that it's more normal to have sensory, physical, mental, or emotional problems than to not have any? The more I learned about special education—and the people around me—the surer I was that the answer was yes.

I have always loved people. I love making friends, and I love helping my friends in whatever ways I can. I must also give off a comfortable vibe because many of the people I have met decided quickly that I was someone they could confide in and seek counsel from.

In college, I loved to listen and help, but sometimes I felt as if I was

Ashley Nance

sharing burdens with so many people that it was hard to keep from buckling under my own. One major source of my friends—and their challenges—was our nightly scripture study group.

Beginning in my first semester of college, I attended a small scripture study group that my friends held nightly a few doors down from my dorm. This group grew and changed and moved to different locations several times over the course of my time at school, and one of the places we met for a time was in my apartment.

After scripture study had ended one night, my roommate pointed out that I had someone to represent just about every high school stereotype she could think of in the group. I realized there was a solid cross section there: we had a preppy type, a few computer geeks, a goth, a couple of populars, and some who were simply happy to be weird, with a few kind-of-normal ones mixed in. I also knew from my conversations with them, though she might not have, that I also had many well-known disabilities represented: Asperger's, bipolar disorder, depression, anxiety, and reactive attachment to name a few.

To me, those labels didn't matter, and maybe that's part of why everyone felt so comfortable coming. To me, diagnoses were—and are—for helping individuals and families understand what they were up against and how to cope with, process, and/or improve their lives based on that understanding. High school stereotypes look at what a person likes to wear or do. Diagnoses look at how a person's body and mind react to the stimulation we call life. As I interacted with these people who met at my apartment each night, I realized that there were more important criteria for grouping people.

If we all had problems, which we do, then the real measure of a person would be their attitude toward those problems. Those of my associates who treated their problems as excuses for not meeting challenges failed. Several of them even failed out of school. Those who treated their problems as mountains to climb and conquer learned and grew from their struggles and succeeded. Maybe they didn't get straight As, but they walked tall with the

97

stature of those who'd done their best. My friends' success was never determined by the severity or nature of the problem, but rather by whether they defined themselves by their challenges or proactively decided how to conquer them so they could be who they wanted to be. This was inspiring and helped me remember to adopt the same policy in my own life.

As my attitude toward disabilities began to change and mature so did the way I interacted with Crystal.

While I was adjusting to being away from home for the first time ever, my family was adjusting to having someone away from home. I was grateful for their Sunday phone calls when everyone at home would take a few minutes to talk to me. I didn't dislike talking to Crystal; in fact, I often used her turn to talk as an opportunity to grab a bite to eat, check my e-mail, or, I'm sorry to say, do some homework.

Talking to her required no active engagement of the mind because as she told me everything that was happening in her life, she almost never paused to listen for a response from me. It was easy, I thought, and maybe a little silly. Sometimes, I would interrupt, usually because what she was saying seemed false or because she was bragging about something she'd said or done that wasn't actually worthy of praise. Getting her to stop so that I could speak wasn't unlike putting on the brakes in a steam engine:

" . . . and I thought it was so funny!"

"Crystal."

"So I laughed and then I was like . . . "

"Crystal."

" . . . How did you do that?'

"*Cryyyyyss . . .* "

"Andhesaidhewouldn'ttellme . . . "

"*tallllllll . . .* "

" . . . becauseitwasasecret. (*deep inhale*) What?"

"Did you tell Mom about this already?"

"Well . . . "

And she would begin again, halting and lurching through actual conversation as long as I insisted on it, until I allowed her to get her train of thought chugging along again so she could eventually make it to the end of the tracks.

At first, I thought of talking to Crystal on the phone as a service that I was providing her. The less I interrupted or expressed any kind of dislike or annoyance toward what she told me, the better the service was for her. The benefit I received from listening was mainly that I knew it made her happy and that God would bless me for trying to be a good sister.

Somewhere inside me, I always knew I could do better than that. She was a person, after all, and people don't tell stories so that they can be ignored. Besides, she was my sister, and family should always treat family better than they would want to be treated. Just because being mostly ignored didn't bother her as much as it would bother me didn't mean that I had an excuse to treat Crystal that way.

As I grew, I decided to be a more actively engaged listener. I would interject with more positive sentiments, such as "fun!" and "good job!" and "she sounds like a good friend!" She could hear these quick things over the sound of her wheels on the rails, and they seemed to improve the experience for both of us. Sometimes, she even responded to what I said.

It turned out she was growing too. One day, she really surprised me:

"I'm sorry. I've been talking for all this time and haven't let you say anything. How are you doing?"

I had to take a moment to catch my breath before I could respond. It was a happy moment for both of us.

Chatting with her online was another adventure. I was sometimes overly critical or blunt in the advice I gave her whenever we chatted online, and I would later feel bad and e-mail her the next day to apologize for being unkind. After the first few of these apology e-mails, she asked me not to send them because she had already forgotten the unkind things I had said, and she was happy to let it stay that way. So if Crystal could remember the tiniest detail for years and was happy to forgive and forget things said to her in impatience less than twenty-four hours before, I wondered, did she forget the more helpful suggestions I made just as efficiently?

Still, I was glad for the opportunity to measure my words, and to grow into a kinder, more thoughtful sister.

I guess the attitude people have toward their negative tendencies really does make a difference, even when one of those people is me.

Shortly before one of my school breaks, my dad told me about a program one of his co-workers had told him about that he thought I might like to participate in while I was home. An organization seeking to support the siblings of children with disabilities was piloting a program called Sibshops, and it was looking for an adult sibling to attend the workshops as a role model that the children could talk to.

I was nervous, but I called the number he gave me, and I was encouraged to hear how excited they were to have me participate. I was really impressed by the program. The venue was unassuming, the atmosphere was personal but professional, and the expectations were age-appropriate. The children were encouraged to talk about their feelings and associate with each other without any judgment of "good" feelings or "bad" feelings.

Even though it wasn't *for* me, I still learned a great deal. I don't know how much I did for the five or six children that came to the group, but they helped me realize how many kids were out there, kids like me, who were trying to be good to a sibling they struggled to understand.

On the last day, the children and their siblings came and participated in carnival games together. I still remember the look on one of the girls' faces when she came in that morning with her brother. I recognized in her eyes the same inner turmoil and poorly suppressed embarrassment I had experienced as a child as well as the contrast of her brother's indifferent gaze as he looked around the room, oblivious to the emotions his mere presence evoked in his sister. I longed for a way to assure her that she was doing great and that it really would get better.

For the first time, I began to think of ways I could help children by sharing my experience so they would know they were not alone. That was when the idea for this book was born.

During the five years I was enrolled in college, I found pieces to the Crystal puzzle literally all over the world. I worked as a tutor in several academic subjects during my semesters at school. When I wasn't in school, I worked at the mall at night and as a substitute teacher's assistant in the daytime. In addition, I worked in various area schools and at Prospect Child and Family Center, where Crystal had gone to preschool years before. I also went to Florida, Spain, and Denmark as a nanny, China as an English teacher, and Taiwan as a religious missionary.

No matter how far I roamed from home, I took my family with me in my heart and mind. And as my passion for serving children with special needs grew, my experiences taught me more about Crystal and about myself.

A few of these experiences really stand out in my mind as being puzzle pieces that shaped my life and my future.

I traveled to China with a volunteer group of college students associated with International Language Programs. We taught preschool classes in teams, first and second grade classes on a rotation, and fifth grade classes individually.

As we got into things, some of my fellow teachers mentioned they had noticed that some of the students seemed to have disabilities of one sort or another. Two of these children were in the same preschool classroom. I didn't notice them at first, and I wondered later whether this might have been because they weren't always allowed to participate.

I was walking around the classroom one morning, passing out paper for an activity, when I noticed two students, a boy and a girl, whom I hadn't seen before. They seemed cheerful, and it didn't occur to me that they might have been at the very back of the room for a reason. When I got to them, one of the Chinese preschool teachers stepped into my way.

"No," she said, motioning with her hands. "*Tā men hěn bèn.*" *No, they are stupid.*

I just stared for a second, trying to process what I had just heard. I looked down at the children. I did notice that the boy looked slightly cross-eyed, once I was looking for something, but the girl was just a little more cheerful and quieter than the average child. I couldn't imagine that either of them had any disability I would consider serious. Even if they did, I wouldn't exclude them from an activity based on their intelligence level.

"It's OK," I said, and I gave them some paper anyway.

The teacher was obviously frustrated, assuming she had been misunderstood, and she looked around the room for reinforcements. My friends and I just went on with the activity as planned. I probably should have felt bad for ruffling the teacher's feathers, but I was just trying not to be angry. *What do you mean, they're stupid? They are children! We came here to teach the children English. If they're children, they qualify!* I was glad she didn't take the papers away. Otherwise, they really would have had a fight on their hands.

My fellow teachers looked at me with questions in their eyes, and I tried to explain as well as I could without interrupting the lesson we'd planned. Meanwhile, the classroom teacher went around trying to find a Chinese teacher who knew English better than she did who could explain the problem to us better than she could.

I knew what she was doing, but I let her look. I didn't know Chinese well enough to explain my feelings to her either, and her search bought the children some participation time with the group for once. Someone tried to show us what the two children had done with their papers, presumably hoping to illustrate by the carelessness of their drawings why they should not be allowed to participate with the others, but they were talking to the wrong people.

Finally, they were able to convince Emily, the director of the school, to come help. That was a relief to me because she and I had already started to become friends. She also had the English vocabulary of at least a three-year-old, which was more than could be said for the other teachers there at the time. Using very simple English and big, sweeping hand motions, I did my best to explain that we did understand what the teacher had said, but we would be happiest to teach all of the children and wished that all of the children be allowed to participate.

I was so relieved when she seemed to understand! As she relayed the message to the Chinese teachers, they seemed more rather than less confused, but at least they knew we understood them. To their credit, they tried to be pleasant with us and allowed us to include everyone, and the children all continued on cheerfully, oblivious to the turmoil the adults around them were working through.

I thought a lot about what it all meant. I had to before my mind could slow down and recover from the explosion it had experienced. It raced back and forth between questions like, *What if their parents knew their efforts to pay for their child's education were spent on a school that didn't want them to participate?* and *Would they even be bothered to see their children treated that way?*

Even though my questions concerned and frustrated me, I realized I was only seeing a very small part of a very big picture. I never faulted them as people, though, for acting the way they did. They were not mean spirited or cruel. It was clear that it was simply the way things were done.

At length, my thoughts turned to how this attitude toward children with disabilities was similar to that prevalent in the United States just a few decades before. If my family had lived in the '50s, for example, Crystal wouldn't have fared very well in school either. There would not have been anyone to play games with her to help develop her motor skills, teach her sign language, or encourage her speech. Crystal's second grade teacher, who complained endlessly about her oddities, would have been closer to the rule than the exception.

I doubt my parents would have sent Crystal away to an institution as many parents did then, regardless of the social pressures to do so that might have existed, but she might have had to stay home rather than attend school with the rest of us. How much greater then would the pressure have been on me and my siblings to be "normal," to excel, and to be strong, smart, kind—to be grown-up? *How must it feel to these parents, who are only allowed one child, to try to raise a child with challenges?*

At last, my mind settled on a new and exciting dream: to learn Chinese, come back to China, and spend my life travelling the country to set up schools for children with special needs that would help them learn the skills they needed to function in society. I would also try to educate educators on how to care for these children, and I would help everyone see what these children could do and grow up to be.

Even if it could just be one school . . .

I wanted to change the world, and I decided that this would be the best way to do it.

However, I also started to suspect that there was more to helping children with disabilities than changing the education system. Could it be that the parents of these children would rather pay for others to educate them—at a boarding school where their children would be separated from them for ten days out of every two weeks while school was in session—than have them home for part of every day? Could it be that they didn't know a better way? Did they see the full value of their roles as parents?

One first grader in my rotation was a particular challenge. He spoke very little, didn't respond well to directions, and often stirred up his classmates by simply finding something random to do that seemed more fun than the activity the teacher had prepared. The teacher responsible for naming him chose "Dameon" because it sounded like "devil" to her, and she couldn't in good conscience name him "Diablo."

The more I learned about Dameon, the more I thought he might have been diagnosed with autism if he had lived in the States. My roommate and best friend, Katrina, and I decided to show him love and acceptance instead of the constant reprimands he got from most of his Chinese and American teachers. We went and played with him and the other children when we could during their playtime and at night when they were getting ready for bed. All of the children seemed to respect us more for the effort we put into loving them.

One night, before classes let out for the evening, Katrina saw Dameon alone outside his classroom, standing on a low ledge around a shallow fountain. She could see the teacher through a nearby window, still teaching his class inside. She got closer and quietly called out to him, asking what he was doing.

His answer was silent, but clear. He met her eyes for a second, and then he looked back at his feet. He shuffled his feet sideways a few times on the ledge, thus moving himself a few inches around the fountain he was facing before he looked up and met her eyes again. He held her gaze as he brought his index finger up to his lips: *Shhh.* Then he looked down again and continued on his way along the ledge.

Message received, Katrina continued on her way back to the dorm to tell me what she had seen. This child was not a problem because he didn't understand the rules; he just saw the arbitrariness of it all and refused to comply. He was, in many ways, smarter than average. Maybe he knew something even the adults didn't know.

When the parents came at the end of the school year to watch their children's special performances, I noticed that Dameon's mother looked tired, but she seemed more than willing to receive his many hugs. It was a huge comfort to me to know that at least he had his mommy.

Even though he was never mine to start with, I felt like I could be at peace to leave him in this world that didn't understand him after seeing the secure attachment and loving relationship he had with his mother. I wanted to be that kind of mother to my children and that kind of sister to Crystal. I also began to wonder whether changing the world needed to be as dramatic as I had first imagined in order to be effective.

Two years later, I was back in a Chinese-speaking country, this time as a missionary. We missionaries were most effective, not to mention safest, when we traveled in pairs, so I was always with at least one other person during my service there. I learned to speak the language quickly, which was a good thing, since it turned out that most of the women I served with were native Chinese speakers who knew little English. One of these was named Yi Ting Liang.

Before I met Yi Ting, I talked to her on the phone. She told me she had heard I was a good and hard worker, so she was excited that we would be serving together in the city of Jia Yi. I told her I was excited too. Then her companion, who would be staying in the city of Gong Shan where they were at the time, got on the phone. She told me she and Yi Ting were friends from back home and were very close. Then she kindly asked me to take good care of her friend. A little surprised by her heartfelt request, I promised I would.

I soon learned why this good woman had asked me to take care of her friend; my new companion was an Asian version of Crystal.

They had so much in common! From the wonderful to the not-so-wonderful, I found that their list of differences was shorter than their list of similarities. Unfortunately, while I consciously compared my new friend to my sister, I unconsciously began to treat her the same way.

One morning, she buckled under the pressure of my high expectations and almost constant corrections, and she dissolved into a puddle of tears. Like a child who'd been sent to her room for something she didn't do, she screamed, "*Wotaoyàn! Wotaoyàn!*" *I hate it!*

My eyes went wide as I finally realized what I was doing and saw how hurtful it was to both of us. I turned from her, went into the bedroom, and fell down to my knees. Now it was my turn to cry. I poured my heart out in prayer, admitting at last to myself and God that my tendency to criticize and correct was a terrible weakness in my character that I wanted to root out.

I prayed to know what to do for Yi Ting and felt impressed to make a promise to never criticize again. No when-absolutely-necessary, no when-it's-serious. I would *never* criticize again. A tall order, to be sure, but I made the promise to Him in prayer and then to Yi Ting. I hugged her and told her that I was sorry, that I loved her, and that I would treat her better from then on.

With God as my helper, I made good on my promise. The rest of our time together was sweet and full of joy. I began to see her strengths more clearly than I saw her weaknesses, and she blossomed and learned once she had been freed from the weight she had carried before. I began to see her talents that I could strive to emulate, and she worked to develop some of my strengths without any prompting from me.

And she loved me. She hugged me, smiled at me, made me food, and wrote me heart-shaped notes of encouragement like I was the best thing that ever happened to her. Anything I tried to do in return seemed small in comparison. It was all so sweet and so genuine that it hurt inside. I couldn't ignore the feeling that this short time with her was only the beginning and that God expected me to apply what I had learned to keep my new promise with every one of His children. Including Crystal.

It wasn't long before this promise was put to the test. While I was away, Crystal had spent some time with my mother's parents, and while she learned some skills from them, they felt their efforts to "fix" her had failed.

Shortly after my mission had concluded, Mom and I decided it would be good for Crystal to move into an apartment near me. We thought she was ready for a dose of independence and that moving out of the house was just the sort of thing that could help her start to become her own person. I was back at school by this time, so there would be plenty of housing within walking distance of my apartment. Crystal could find a job and learn to live with roommates and do her own grocery shopping and gain experience living on her own, all within a safe distance from a responsible family member. Mom and I would help her get moved in and set up together.

An advantage for me was that the car the state had helped buy for Crystal, back when we thought she could learn how to drive, would come with her, which would help us both get to the store and run other necessary errands around town. It sounded and felt like the perfect fit for everyone.

All three of us were excited to see where this new turn in her life would take her.

I also reconnected with a young man during my semester at home who turned my understanding of disability and of my sister upside down.

I had first met Joe far away from home at a church-sponsored dance. I wanted to ask him to dance with me because he seemed like he was mostly watching and like he might be lonely, but by the time I got the opportunity, I realized it would be more fun for both of us if I just sat down and talked to him.

You see, he would be sitting either way, and it was easier to communicate with a person in a loud room if you were sitting by them rather than standing far enough out in front of them to keep your toes from being rolled over. He rode around in a motorized wheelchair—like he owned the place—and his hands bent a little funny and his legs seemed unusually thin. I soon found out that even though he *looked* like someone with a disability, he didn't *talk* like someone with a disability, or *act* like someone with a disability, or even *think* like someone with a disability.

I was amazed at how much Joe and I had in common. We talked and talked for probably an hour. My new friend wanted to be a filmmaker, and he loved Halloween costumes and his family, especially his mother. I found him fascinating and fun in every way, and I felt myself quite fortunate to have met him at all. I was even more excited when we regained contact again later so that our friendship could continue. Even though years had passed in between the times we were able to talk in person, I had thought about him often.

When Mom brought Crystal and me out west so I could continue school and Crystal could begin her life as a semi-independent adult, we caravaned with Joe. This way, we could take turns riding with him and keep him company on the long trip, which was important because he was the only one who could drive his specially adapted vehicle. That road trip was one of the most fun, edifying, and educational experiences I have ever had.

Joe told me that his disorder was incredibly rare, something like one in a million, and that there was no reason why he should have lived, but he had. He told me about his memories on road trips with his mother, with whom he had an especially close relationship. He told me about his siblings and his parents and his movies and his music, and I felt like my reality was being rewritten in front of my eyes.

He told me that he had hated going to IEP meetings while he was growing up and that he didn't like talking about his disability with people at school. He couldn't identify with other students with disabilities because he felt none of the anger toward his condition that many of them felt, or the entitlement to adaptations that so many of them seemed bent on fighting for. At the same time, he wasn't insecure about his needs, in denial that he was different, or bashful about considerately asking for the accommodations he needed to function in a world built for walking adults.

The biggest difference I found about Joe was that his special needs were needs to him, not excuses. And here I was, learning how to put children with special needs in categories so they could be best served by the system, trying to define this man who knew no classifications. No box was big enough to contain the awesomeness that was Joe.

"I've never had anything I wanted to do that I couldn't do." That one sentence has visited me in times of trouble and helped guide my vision of strangers, of Crystal, and of myself.

Could Crystal ever feel this way about herself?

Could we ever think about her in this way?

Could she if we didn't? Could we if she didn't?

Eventually, I gave up trying to define him, and I focused instead on learning from him, enjoying our friendship, and introducing my awesome friend to all of my other friends at college.

Meanwhile, I was learning that I wouldn't have an easier time trying to "fix" Crystal than my grandparents had. Crystal's first attempt at independent living was a surprising wake-up call for the family and, I think, for her. Left to make her own choices, she stayed up late reading her books and watching movies and TV shows with her roommates, even when they included obviously objectionable content. Then she slept in late, sometimes even into the afternoon.

Afraid of calling strangers to ask for a ride, she didn't go to church on weeks when her less orthodox roommates didn't go, because she would have gotten lost if she tried to walk by herself. She also took advantage of her roommates' generosity, sometimes to a level that made me wonder if I should apologize for her. She also didn't feel the urgency of getting a job that I hoped she would because the state was paying for her existence through Social Security Income (SSI) funds.

I tried to help her out and talk to her as much as I could, and I had her over for dinner at least once a week, but my full course load—and increasingly complicated social life—made it difficult for me to do much more than that. Still, from her perspective, aside from the shirtless poster of David Beckham in her room that her roommate refused to take down, life was pretty good for Crystal.

Before long, I had a regular movie night going with Joe. While I don't usually go for PG-13 movies, I let Joe convince me to share a favorite or two of his because he really enjoyed picking out movies for people, and I had come to trust him.

For one such movie night, my roommates, some friends, Crystal, and I heaved Joe down into the basement movie room under the apartment manager's office and prepared to enjoy one of Joe's favorites with great anticipation.

It was a well-crafted suspense film, and I was working hard to believe Joe's promise that it was not a horror film when one of the characters suddenly stabbed another with a knife. We all jumped, which was the desired effect, but Crystal also screamed and then dissolved into sobs. She cried and cried like her heart would break.

I had never seen her so hysterical. Someone stopped the movie while I hurried over to hug and comfort her.

"Joe!" I called out.

"I didn't know she would react this way," he said in his defense, albeit apologetically.

I knew he loved film almost more than life and that he had a strict no-spoiler policy when sharing movies with people who hadn't seen them before, but I was still mad at him. I had already ascertained that Crystal had developed a crush on the character that had been stabbed, which added an additional level of drama to the situation. I knew there was no way Joe could have guessed that movies and books were Crystal's preferred reality, but I still felt that a scene as violent as that called for some kind of forewarning.

Joe and all my friends and roommates were trying to help Crystal calm down, but she just cried and cried. I wasn't upset at her for making a scene because I knew she wasn't making it up; she was responding just the way I would if someone had been actually murdered ten feet in front of my face.

When it was beyond obvious that the damage was done and people started to offer to take Crystal home, Joe caved. He said to Crystal, trying hard to comfort her but with great pain in his eyes, "I don't usually do this, but I'll tell you that he doesn't die."

The level of compassion required for him to disclose this was not lost on me, and I was grateful that he was man enough to make this concession. Joe encouraged her to continue watching so she could see that the character would be OK, and this seemed to help at last. I think the idea that Crystal might not finish watching the movie and instead leave hating it if Joe didn't do something was even more abhorrent to him than the idea of breaking his no-spoiler rule.

With this reassurance from Joe and kind words from the rest of us, Crystal agreed to continue watching. The character was indeed all right in the end, but I was never quite sure what made Joe sadder: not warning Crystal ahead of time, or giving in and telling her something that the movie should have been allowed to tell her.

He and I became very close that year and spent a lot of time together. After a while, I realized I didn't feel any romantic attraction to him at all, and that bothered me a little.

I tried to determine why this might be. Could it be because of his wheel-chair, or because his body was disproportionate? Was it because Walmart had relational-violence fired him, which made me wonder whether he would be able to get or keep a good enough job for long enough so that I could stay home with children? Was it because I wondered whether or not he could even have children or because I worried that his condition was hereditary? Was it because I was worried that he'd need too much help when he got older?

I had a sincere heart-to-heart with myself about this, and I ultimately concluded that none of these uncertainties would keep me from wanting to be with him forever if I wanted to be with him. None of these things made him less attractive to me than I already found him based on how he thought, talked, and acted. I honestly had more trouble relating to his hobbies and religious/political philosophies than any of these things, and if he were still him in a completely different, perfectly typical body, I still would not have been attracted to him. Relieved, I laid the issue to rest and returned to just enjoying his friendship and college life in general.

These same ponderings, however, led to other unsettling thoughts. If I were male, would I like Crystal? I loved the same movies and music, and I could deal with her books. Enough of our interests were the same that we would have plenty to do together and talk about. It made me sad to think about, but I realized that the turn-offs for me in her case were parts of her personality that I associated with her disability. Specifically, her carelessness toward her physical appearance, her tendency to read all day unless compelled to do something else, and her apparent laziness toward life in general. It made me sad to have to wonder whether anyone good enough for me to consider going on a date with would ever want to date my sister.

But I had no trouble imagining what kind of guy *would* want to hook up with her.

During my years away from home, I had several nightmares that Crystal was pregnant with disturbing frequency. What little variation there was between the dreams had mostly to do with where we were and how close Crystal was to the time of birth. In every dream, she was perfectly calm with no sense of anxiety about the difficulty of childbirth or regret about—or even consciousness of—the mistake she had made that led her to that point.

I always fought the urge to wonder whether she even knew she was preg-nant, and I did wonder whether she fully understood how a person got to be pregnant or what happened to a woman between being pregnant and holding a cute baby in her arms. I also always tried not to think about whether or not she could handle childbirth at all, because it frightened me to imagine how to help her when she was as afraid as I imagined she would be while in labor.

In these dreams, she was also never married. The man responsible was always known but never named, and he was never around or conceivably concerned. There were always many family members around, wondering what to do with the coming child, but there was never any discussion about whether Crystal could care for the child herself because it was understood generally that she could not. We talked to each other and not to her, though she was sometimes present if not at least within earshot. There didn't seem to be much to say though, just this urgent, overwhelming question that pressed into every particle and wave in that dream: "What do we do?"

And each time, I was personally focused on how I could help, and I usu-ally came to the conclusion that it would fall to me to adopt and raise the child myself.

After several years of this, I confided my concerns about this reoccurring dream to my father who, to my surprise, was not at all surprised. He said he had similar concerns, and his worries added new levels of reality to mine.

He told me that he guessed that all a guy would have to do is smile sweetly at Crystal as he asked her to swear not to tell her family because they "just wouldn't understand." Then he could sweep her romantically off her feet, marry her, and ride off into the sunset, and she would never be heard from again.

This was a huge reason why Dad had taken such great pains to coach and encourage Crystal rather than make decisions for her and attempt to force her to comply. This had always annoyed me a little, but now I understood that it was because he didn't want to push her away so effectively with his disappointment that she wouldn't want to invite us to the wedding, so to speak.

Now this made more sense, but the fact that he—the most intelligent and spiritual person I knew—and I had come to the same conclusions on our own validated my own feelings and made them more frightening. If Dad thought it was worth being concerned about, then I couldn't convince myself that it could never happen. And as much as I liked to live in reality, thinking of this worst-case scenario as an impossibility was a fantasy I wasn't quite ready to let go of.

But life doesn't tend to care much about what you think you're ready for.

That year was full of boy drama for me. During my mission, I had opened my heart to the possibility that Matthew might not be destined to be my husband. So, when I returned, I tried to keep my mind open to other possibilities. The result was that I had more dates in one year than I'd had in my whole life up to that point and, in one month in particular, more serious conversations about my relationship status than any girl should be subjected to in so short a time.

One of my suitors, whom I had met in New York, asked me during one of our conversations whether he'd ever told me that Crystal had asked to be his girlfriend once. Surprised, since to my knowledge she hadn't had a conversation with him, much less spent any quality time with him, I asked to hear the story.

He told me she had first asked if he remembered who she was, and he responded that he knew she was my sister. Then she'd said, "Since you and Ashley used to go out, I was wondering if you would consider going out with me?"

I was floored. I thought even Crystal, with her 150-page love story paradigm, knew better than to pull something like that. He laughed as he recalled their conversation and said he'd declined as kindly as he could, and she'd gone off by herself and probably cried. I apologized, and he just laughed some more and said I shouldn't feel bad because he was just curious whether or not she had told me about it, and he wanted me to know if she hadn't.

I tried to talk to her about it later, but it seemed like my suggestions on how to avoid scaring guys away fell on stubbornly deaf ears. Sometimes, I wondered if she ever listened to me at all. She tried to pick up guys a few times while she lived her new independent life, with similar results every time. She always told me she felt embarrassed, but it didn't seem to deter her from trying again.

One time, the guy she tried to ask out was my boyfriend.

With all of the emotional roller coasters I had been on with guys, I had never actually committed to being anyone's girlfriend before. I'd been on dates, talked for hours on the phone, and exchanged letters and e-mails, but I had always made a concerted effort to be sure all parties concerned were well aware that I was not anyone's yet.

Then finally, in my final year at college, I found *The One*. Really, I found him again. David Nance, my good friend from freshman year, re-entered my life, and I knew after our first date that I would never be the same again.

A month or so into our official courtship, Crystal asked to talk to David alone. He agreed. Once she had him to herself, she confessed her love for him and asked if he would consider dating her instead. He told me later, as I tried to keep my chin off the floor, that he had kindly declined, explaining that he'd already chosen his Brayton girl and that there was someone else for her somewhere. She had taken it fairly well, and they came back together to where the rest of us were talking and eating.

David's attitude toward Crystal helped me not feel quite so embarrassed about what she had done. He treated her as a person, one who he knew had difficulties functioning socially on the same level as those around her, and he was sad to have made her sad, even though he hadn't done anything wrong and didn't have any regrets about how he had responded.

This was such a contrast to the other's laughing, ridiculing response. It made me grateful all over again that David and I had found each other, and it gave me reassurance that if we did end up together forever, he would be a good father for our children, whether they had disabilities or not.

Two weeks after this, Crystal, David, and I went on a road trip to visit my mother's parents and her sister's family. Crystal didn't act embarrassed or make another attempt during the trip or ever again.

Every time I put together a few more pieces, the puzzle just grew!

By the end of that year, David and I were married, and we continued on the incredible journey we call life together.

∞ 6 ∞

With God, All Things Are Possible

The summer semester after I married David, I prepared to present my portfolio to a board of professors, professionals, and others interested in students entering the field. This was the last step I had to take before I began my student teaching experience in the fall, at the conclusion of which, I would officially have my bachelor's degree and teaching certificate. Because my degree was a blended certificate, my experience would include working with both a special education teacher and a mainstream classroom teacher at the school I was assigned to.

I only recognized a couple of the eight members of my portfolio review board, but I was more excited than nervous. Compiling the portfolio itself had been stressful, but I felt prepared to present, and I was excited for the opportunity to talk about the things I had learned and done in the five years since I chose my major.

It felt great to know the answers to all of the questions they asked me. These were professionals, well-respected and knowledgeable people, and they seemed pleased with my answers. I shared experiences about children I had learned to see with my heart and adults with no verbal skills that I had learned to respect rather than fear or pity, and I also shared my dreams about being the kind of educator or specialist I would want serving my own child.

I realized as we went along that this was more than a presentation. It was more even than a job interview. It was a life interview. These people wanted to know if in ten or twenty years they would be proud to see me at my work knowing I was trained in the EC/SE program at their school and, more importantly, that I was still serving with love and seeing with my heart.

When they finished their questions, they talked among themselves for some time while I waited outside the room before calling me back in to present me with their decision and written comments. When I returned, they expressed their faith in me and gratitude for being part of my journey.

The thrill I experienced as I listened was indescribable. The last one to comment was a dad whose daughter had multiple disabilities. He had tears in his eyes as he told me I gave him hope that the future of his child was bright with educators like me entering the field. I could not have been more honored by those words, or more humbled. I was just doing my best to see people as people, no matter what their needs were, and treat them the way I would want to be treated myself. It was a profound moment for me to realize how desperately the world I was entering needed the skills I was working to develop, and I determined to continue working to develop these skills and serve with them for the rest of my life, no matter what profession my path led me to.

And so it was with a cheerful smile and a confident stride that I walked across the stage to accept my diploma, ready to close the door on my familiar university career and enter the world of the classroom teacher. I expected to learn a great deal about teaching, being a teacher, and my personal strengths and weaknesses as an educator during my student teaching experience, but I didn't expect that it would guide me to people, such as Mrs. Susan VanFrank, who would teach me more about Crystal.

Mrs. VanFrank, the mainstream first grade teacher I worked with, went the extra mile to take a budding teacher under her wing in order to show me the best of the methods and strategies she had learned over the course of her thirty-year teaching career. She took interest in my family too, especially Crystal. Perhaps this was easier for her because she herself had a son with a disability.

She had a daughter in medical school and a son, whom I'll call Will, in an adult group home with others with intellectual disabilities. She loved to talk and brag about both of them. She said that there had been difficult times in her life, but she had learned the value of the motto she frequently repeated: "Blessed are the flexible for they shall not be bent out of shape."

I listened with rapt attention to her stories because I was interested in her personally and because so much of what she had learned from her child applied to my relationship with Crystal. I wanted to feel about Crystal like Mrs. VanFrank felt about her son.

Two instances stand out in my mind as particularly significant:

Around Halloween, which was Mrs. VanFrank's favorite holiday, she had gone to her son's place, as she often did, for a visit. This time, she brought one of her favorite books to read to her son and his roommates.

As she described the scene, absolute glee shone from her eyes.

She told them she had brought a story to read and that they should sit so they all could see the pictures. They eagerly did so and anxiously waited for her to begin. She put everything she had into that story, all the expressions, character voices, drama, and suspense that the author could have asked for in its retelling. These young men hooted and laughed and begged for more. She agreed to one encore and then said she had to go but that she would come read again some other time.

The light in her eyes dimmed a little as she told me what happened next.

Her son stopped her by pulling on her shirt. Looking at her face intently, he pointed to her ("Mom"), to himself ("Will"), and to the door ("go home"). Then again, "Mom, Will, go home." She told him no, he had to stay with his friends and have a good time, but Mom would come another day to play. She knew he was getting what he needed where he was: companionship, some independence, and safety. The very best she could give Will was love since both of his aging parents were working, and she could do that without bringing him home and without losing all that had been or could be gained from his housing arrangement. Still, it was always hard to explain again why Mom had to go and Will had to stay.

I didn't understand fully why that touched me so much then, but I'm starting to now. I wanted to be that happy to be with Crystal and that willing to interact with her where she was, rather than trying to make her grow up as quickly as possible. I also wanted to love her in such a way that I would be sad to be separated from her, and I wanted to be willing to let her learn how to be on her own at the same time. How would she grow otherwise?

The other gem Mrs. VanFrank shared with me came from a book she read called *When Bad Things Happen to Good People* by Harold S. Kushner. She learned that the grief cycle doesn't only occur when a loved one dies, it happens whenever something expected is lost.

For parents of a child with a disability, this initially means grieving over the loss of the typical child and the typical parenting experience that they have expected to have, but it also continues throughout that child's life. Every time a milestone or opportunity is missed, the grief cycle must be gone through again.

Often, the parent may be processing different stages of several cycles simultaneously, such as when a parent doesn't have a chance to get over receiving a diagnosis for her child's disability before she realizes that her child will likely never walk without assistance. The steps (Denial, Isolation, Anger, Bargaining, Depression, Acceptance) may not always be passed through in order, and some may need to be revisited more than once. Some cycles of the grief process may take an entire lifetime to get through, while others may require only a minute or two.

For example, Mrs. VanFrank remembered feeling sad when she realized that Will would never have the experience of going to the prom. But immediately, she thought of what that meant: No prom meant no date. No date meant no girl, and no girl meant no unexpected grandchildren in need of support! In less than a minute, she had already reached closure, and she breathed a happy sigh of relief that she didn't have to worry about Will going to the prom.

The understanding of this process was *huge* for me, and I have been able to help many in my own family as well as others by sharing this with them. Some of the uncomfortable feelings that the family members of people with disabilities experience are emotions of grief, and furthermore, grief isn't something that a parent, sibling, or anyone should feel ashamed for experiencing because it's not optional. Grief is even a healthy part of getting to know the individual with the disability, understanding what their challenges mean, and growing as a person.

In the years since I experienced this revelation, I have learned that many of us go through our whole lives in denial, feeling that it wouldn't be right to be sad because there's no one to blame, and the individual with a disability is certainly not at fault for any inconvenience caused, so it's just better to go on as if nothing is wrong. That perspective is unhealthy, unrealistic, and, I think, harmful to both parties. The sooner a person owns their feelings and submits to the grief process, the sooner that person can get through it and rest in closure.

I also later learned that not all of Crystal's quirks come from her disability.

My mother's older sister Tami married Chris, who served as an officer in the Air Force, and we consequently had very little contact with their family over the years.

My last year of college was her son's first, so I had made an effort to spend some time with my now grown-up cousin. It turned out that was a good thing for him and a good thing for me. He got Southern food from my roommate and asked at least one of my friends out on a date, and I was impressed with the strength of his faith and the goodness of his heart. His goodness rekindled inside of me a desire to reconnect with the rest of his family.

Fast forward a couple years. I was living in New York with my husband and baby boy at my parents' house when Uncle Chris accepted a job teaching at a university in Potsdam. Their home was only a four-hour drive away from ours, which was the closest they had lived to us since I was four years old. Aunt Tami, who loved a clean house but didn't have the energy or wrist strength to clean a whole house by herself anymore, offered to pay me to come and help her. David and I talked it over and decided I could go.

It was a challenge to balance giving enough attention to my seven-month-old and cleaning the house, even with the assistance of my aunt, but it was all well worth the trip. For the first time in my life, I got the chance to see my four oldest cousins through their mother's eyes, and with all the tension inherent in interacting with my mother's side of the family, this chance was priceless.

But I learned something else too. I learned that Crystal was a lot like Aunt Tami.

Tami and Crystal shared the same laugh and many of the same quirky facial expressions. They also shared a tendency to stay up late reading and sleep in late. They both loved to talk, enjoyed shopping, cared about the people around them, desired the approval of others, and loved few things more than when their man came through like a knight in shining armor to save the day for his precious princess.

I was surprised they had so much in common, and a little embarrassed that this surprised me. I was a little ashamed to admit to myself that I had never considered the possibility that my siblings and I might have inherited some personality traits from my mother's side of the family. When I realized that I had associated some of the traits I saw in Aunt Tami directly with Asperger's syndrome, the wheels started to turn in my head.

Aunt Tami clearly did not have Asperger's syndrome, yet she and Crystal had many things in common. If these traits came from Crystal's inborn personality rather than from her disability, what other quirks were just from her being her? I could almost see my past being rewritten before my eyes. The conclusion: Crystal and I had both blamed more of her mistakes on her Asperger's than we should have.

This realization had both positive and negative implications, but it marked a major shift in my attitude toward Crystal. It also marked the end of the bargaining and blame stage of a grief cycle I didn't even know I was in.

Years later, at the time I submitted my proposal for this book to my publisher, Crystal was attending Scenic View Academy, a special school for adults with learning disabilities. Mom and Dad had hoped that Scenic View would be the bridge between her almost totally dependent existence and the somewhat independent lifestyle we all hoped she could maintain on her own someday.

But despite her promises that she would only date casually and not immediately pair off with someone, within two weeks, she was already steadily dating a boy and, by extension, his emotionally abusive and controlling helicopter mom. "By extension" describes the situation perfectly because Crystal's boyfriend lived with his mother off campus, and neither he nor Crystal could drive, so his mom was literally with them almost every minute they were together.

He wasn't a good influence on Crystal, but his mother was worse, and whenever she learned that any of us objected to something Crystal was doing with them, she simply encouraged Crystal not to listen to us.

Crystal told us she loved him, but the way she talked about him and behaved around him made it obvious to the rest of us that she mostly loved having someone's hand to hold. This hand holding quickly progressed to kissing (something she had told him she didn't want to do until after marriage), an engagement ring, and wedding dress shopping, all while her family members all over the country frantically searched for new ways to try to convince her to put on the brakes!

My parents prayed and my mother agonized day and night, but they didn't feel right about taking Crystal out of school against her will and bringing her home. The whole point of her being there was to learn to be independent, and plucking her out of her circumstances wouldn't change her heart. Besides, part of being independent was learning from your own mistakes.

Remember that e-mail I received?

This boy's mother saw the opportunity for her son to get married like a beacon glowing in the night, and she was pursuing the course that led to his wedding day with more diligence and less consideration for the opposing forces at play than an old steam engine. To her, Crystal's family had become an obstacle to overcome or, failing that, avoid. So, she was intentionally, systematically, and even self-righteously working to pull Crystal away from her family, her counselors, her therapists, and anyone else who might try to derail the master plan. I wish I were exaggerating, but I'm not.

As Crystal's relationship reached an almost unbelievable level of ridiculousness, my parents asked my siblings and me to each take a day of the week each week and call Crystal to just talk to her. My parents hoped that daily contact from family members would help remind her of our love for her and keep our ever-impressionable Crystal from slipping away from us entirely, even if we couldn't keep her from making the unwise decisions she stubbornly continued to make.

Meanwhile, we prayed. And by "we" I don't mean just the seven of us (including my husband) on the call list, I mean our whole extended family on both sides. We asked everyone to pray, and eventually, my parents called a special family fast for Crystal on a Sunday. We found strength in our faith and in each other as we sought God's help for this soul we all loved. It brought us together, and it helped me love Crystal more.

Then the emotional image of her I held in my mind began to change.

I no longer saw her as a feather, rendered helpless by the disability she was born with and had no control over, tossed in the wind and blown about by the most salient influence. No, I had learned better than that.

Now I could see that she had more in common with the friends whom I had recently tried to help out of abusive relationships than with Loren who parroted profanities on the after-school bus. Loren didn't resist because he didn't see any danger. My friends did see the danger, but it didn't frighten them. They didn't have learning disabilities, but their impairment had the potential of harming them more than any medical diagnoses because it injured their very souls.

I had come to realize that my friends didn't leave their relationships because they didn't want what they needed more than they wanted what they had. With a heavy heart, I began to see Crystal like that too: a young lady learning to choose whether to stand firm against the wind or allow herself to be blown around by it. She was choosing between light and dark, the path of least resistance and the uphill hike to a better life, which is a choice that each of us has to make at some point in our lives.

As I prayed for her safety, I felt an assurance that she would be all right.

Very soon after our family fast day, I got a surprising phone call from my mother. She was elated. Without anyone telling her to, Crystal had arranged to have her boyfriend meet her at her counselor's office where, with the protective presence of her counselor there to back her up if necessary, she broke up with him and gave him back his ring.

I could hardly believe my ears.

I got the story again from Crystal, with the usual cheer back in her voice, later that day. By then, there was more of the story to be told. She had told him why she was breaking up with him, and he said, as he had said other times when she had objected to one thing or another, that the problems she mentioned were all things he could "work on."

That had been enough before, but not this time. She said he just looked dazed and confused and that he didn't say much. She had exulted in her success, but later that day when she went back to her room after class, he was waiting for her. He tried to talk to her and keep her from going inside, but she refused to discuss it and tried to push past—I imagined her steam engine face—and he raised his hand up like he might hit her. Fortunately, by the grace of God, a therapist walking by saw the whole thing and intervened to keep Crystal safe. As it turned out, the therapist's testimony was enough evidence to justify suspending Crystal's now ex-boyfriend from the school.

She could tell when he was reunited with his mother because they started calling and texting her incessantly. A little sweet persuasion had always worked before, after all. They even tried to call from other family members' and friends' phones to try to get her to answer, but she never did. His mom even called my parents' house and tried to talk to my dad about it—the thought that he might help her contact Crystal made me laugh—which allowed my dad the opportunity to assure her that Crystal had made her choice clear to them already in his calm, unmovable way. This decreased the frequency of their calls to Crystal, but only slightly. After a day or two of this, Mom and Liz helped Crystal block their phone numbers.

Crystal never looked back, and the whole family, united in faith and love, did a spiritual happy dance. The dancing slowed somewhat once it came out that her boyfriend had been even worse for her—and to her—than we had suspected, but we were hopeful that she had now learned that there was more to life, and to love, than having a hand to hold. We were hopeful that she had really learned the lessons she told us she had learned and that she had passed through the dangerous trial of fire and into a new day.

Something else happened inside of me. Something had settled down and came to rest, like a child going to sleep. I realized I had arrived at a place I didn't know I was going to.

It was a place called "closure."

Crystal has a learning disability. Crystal will always have a learning disability. And that's OK. The Crystal Puzzle was still incomplete. There were still many things I didn't understand about Asperger's syndrome, about Crystal's personality, about my family, and about myself. But I was at peace.

A few weeks later, at my mother's request, I attended a family open house event at Scenic View. Mom wanted someone to attend, and since I was living within two hours' drive of the school at the time, I agreed to drive down to be there for Crystal to represent her family.

In one of the workshops I attended, I was able to share what I had learned about the mourning process with the parents attending with me, which seemed to bring some peace to their souls as well. Another workshop I attended added hope to my peace. It was taught by one of the teachers, who was married with children and had a successful job there at the school, and who also happened to have Asperger's syndrome.

He talked about the "systems" he had memorized to help him deal with various social situations. For example, while he was growing up, he had a system to avoid being bullied on the school bus and another system to avoid upsetting his mother. Afterward, I asked him about relationship systems, and he gave me some ideas for systems that could help Crystal avoid much of her trouble with boys.

He also taught the class that individuals with disabilities on the autism spectrum could usually be expected to act as if they were two-thirds their chronological age in terms of social and emotional development; however, research has shown that this particular discrepancy between them and their peers doesn't last forever, because while typical minds reach the end of their social and emotional development at about age twenty-seven, minds with autism never stop developing. So, in that way, these individuals will eventually match and even surpass their peers.

This revelation was curiously comforting to me. I did the math and realized that two-thirds of Crystal's age would make her about fourteen—too young for a boyfriend and *definitely* too young to get married.

Crystal and I happened to cross paths with Crystal's ex-boyfriend between events. She sucked in her breath and ducked inside the doorway of a nearby classroom. Surprised, I asked her why she did that. She said she didn't want him to see her.

"Why not?" I asked.

"I don't know."

I guessed she was afraid that she could be convinced to date him again, but she said that wasn't quite it, but she couldn't put her finger on what it was.

Honestly, it was comforting for me to see she had learned that some people were toxic and should be actively avoided. When we saw him again later, there were no rooms nearby so she just turned her back and hurried away in the opposite direction.

The third time we saw him, he was not alone. I was disgusted to see that he was already dating another girl. Crystal didn't seem hurt that she had been so quickly replaced, but she did think it was odd. We both agreed that we felt sorry for the girl, especially when we saw that his mother was still as close to his heels as ever. None of them said a word to either of us.

I tried to help Crystal feel better, or at least more at ease, so I talked to her a little about what she had learned. I listened with interest to her response, especially what she wanted to never happen again. Then we found more cheerful things to talk about, and we turned our thoughts to enjoying the food, the beautiful weather, and each other.

I talked to Mom about what I had learned at the open house event, from the mourning stages to the ex-evasion. I also told her how at peace I felt about Crystal and how hopeful I felt about her future now that the boyfriend drama had passed.

At peace and hopeful, but still with room to grow.

Crystal went home during a break from school shortly after the open house. Soon after she returned to Scenic View, we were all disappointed to learn that she had gone back on all of her boyfriend-related promises again and was dating someone steadily.

I was angry and hurt. She had talked to this guy while she was home, and she and I had talked over the phone about all the red flags we could see and how he was showing no signs of actual love. She had agreed with me enthusiastically, even adding supporting evidence to my own observations based on what she had told me. But when the benefits of having a willing boyfriend were so easily attainable and right in front of her face, she chose the hand to hold over the alone time required to wait for a better option.

I was angry that she had failed herself again and that she hadn't learned all the things I had hoped she'd learned after all. I was also hurt because some of the promises that she had made and broken had been made directly to me.

Sometime during the months that followed, I volunteered to help serve food after a funeral for someone who had attended our congregation at church but whom I had not personally met. My husband watched our two children so I could help. I arrived early to help make sure all was in order before I sat down to listen to the service.

The woman who had passed had been sick and in a great deal of pain when she died, and all of her family members seemed to agree that, while they missed her, they were grateful she could finally rest from her physical difficulties. The family members who spoke at the service shared fun and tender stories about the departed, and a spirit of reverent peace filled the chapel as they shared their feelings that they would be reunited with her again someday.

Then a man, whom I hadn't been able to see well from where I was seated until he stood up, made his way to the pulpit. He stood straight and tall, and he seemed to almost float as he walked. His head was shaved bald, and he was wearing what I recognized from my time as a missionary in Taiwan as the robe of a Buddhist monk.

My heart beat faster as the clanging and chanting of rituals at Buddhist monasteries I had passed on my bike filled my ears. I tried to calm myself, embarrassed that I felt such great alarm before the man, who had every right to be there, had even begun to speak. He stood perfectly straight and calmly slid his hand into the pocket of his robe, pulled out a white sheet of paper, unfolded it, spread it out on the top of the pulpit, and began to read the thoughts he had prepared.

As he read, my heart began to change. He told us that his older sister had a special way about her that allowed her to love him and still treat him as if he were better. This had always inspired him to live up to that high, though unspoken, praise. He told us that he had been concerned that his devoutly Christian family would shun him when he ultimately decided to devote the rest of his life to walking the path of a Buddhist monk, but they instead expressed their love and support for him when they learned of his decision.

This particular sister went a few steps further than that by asking him questions and even buying books about Buddhism to help her understand the path he had chosen and its significance to him. He said she had never judged him or withheld her love, and he missed her very much. Then he folded up his paper, returned it to the inside of his robe, and quietly resumed his seat by his family.

All of this from a man I had judged without ever having met him before.

There is something about funerals that makes you rethink your life.

I thought about the things I did and didn't have in common with the woman whose life and memory was honored that day. I was also the oldest sister in my family, and I also had a sibling who had made choices that disappointed me.

But if it were me in that coffin, would Crystal stand and say that I had always loved her and saw the very best in her? Would she say that I didn't judge her for the decisions she'd made that I didn't agree with? She would say many sweet and wonderful things about me, for she was a sweet and wonderful person, but I was sure that none of those items would be on the list.

I resolved to do better, and I wrote my resolution in my journal. As I prayed for God's help, I felt that He was pleased with my goal and would help me achieve it. These feelings overflowed my heart, and I found it difficult to sing the closing hymn through my tears.

After the service, I busied myself with serving food to the family. I was grateful that this man, this brother, had stayed to eat with the family so that I could thank him for his comments. He smiled genuinely when I did, and he said he was pleased to hear that he had been of help.

Since that day, I have worked hard to love Crystal better and have made significant progress, but the journey to greatness is never a short one, so I still have a long way to go. Still I am sure that, with God as my helper, I will get there someday. I will forever be grateful to the Buddhist monk who reminded me to love my sister the way Jesus would in my place.

Love is the best medicine.

Since that day, not so long ago now, Crystal has broken up with her boyfriend and is taking another break from Scenic View. This time, she is living near me so she can come help me around the house as much as I need so that David can work hard on his doctoral studies while we await the imminent arrival of our third child.

Today, while I've been typing in my room, Crystal's been putting away dishes and cooking potatoes for us to have with dinner. Her willing, cheerful help has been invaluable as I learn to take it easy and eat and drink as much as I need to keep my baby and myself healthy while meeting the other demands of family life. We talk and joke together, and we enjoy each other's company. Once the baby is born and other help is sufficient, she may return to Scenic View or get a job in town here. Ultimately, it will be up to her.

So, while this book draws to its close, the story of the Crystal Puzzle is far from over. There are still many things I don't understand about Asperger's syndrome, about Crystal's personality, about my family, and about myself. But what I do know is enough for now. I am happy, and so is Crystal. The puzzle is still incomplete, but the pieces that have come together so far are forming recognizable scenes.

And the picture is truly beautiful.

Appendix 1

Recommended General Reading ↺

Child Behavior: The Classic Child Care Manual from the Gesell Institute of Human Development by Frances L. Ilg, Louise Bates Ames, and Sidney M. Baker

Diagnostic and Statistical Manual of Mental Disorders: DSM-IV-TR by the American Psychiatric Association

Ordinary Families, Special Children: A Systems Approach to Childhood Disability by Milton Seligman and Rosalyn Benjamin Darling

Parenting with Love and Logic: Teaching Children Responsibility by Foster W. Cline and Jim Fay

Pretending to be Normal: Living with Asperger's Syndrome by Liane Holliday Willey

"The 5 Stages of Loss and Grief" by Julie Axelrod: http://psychcentral.com/lib/2006/the-5-stages-of-loss-and-grief/

The Mother's Almanac by Marguerite Kelly and Elia Parsons

The Mother's Almanac Goes to School by Marguerite Kelly

When Bad Things Happen to Good People by Harold S. Kushner

Information about the Autism Spectrum ⌀

Asperger's Syndrome by Ami Klin PhD, Fred R. Volkmar MD, and Sara S. Sparrow PhD

Asperger's Syndrome: A Guide for Parents and Professionals by Tony Attwood

"Is Being Female Protective Against Autism?" by Emily Willingham: http://www.forbes.com/sites/emilywillingham/2013/02/25/being-female-protective-against-autism/

Information about Sensory Integration Disorder (Sensory Processing Disorder) ⌀

Basic Diagnostic Checklist:

http://www.brainbalancecenters.com/2012/04/signs-and-symptoms-of-sensory-processing-disorder/

Sensory Processing Disorder Foundation: http://www.spdfoundation.net/about-sensory-processing-disorder.html

The Out-of-Sync Child: Recognizing and Coping with Sensory Processing Disorder by Carol Kranowitz

Other Supplements ⌀

Sibshops website: http://www.siblingsupport.org/sibshops

"Hand In Hand" (ballet dance): http://www.youtube.com/watch?v=UTr-b6i7gJAk

Works Cited ✍

Pearson, Carol Lynn and Reid N. Nibley. "I'll Walk with You." Intellectual Reserve, Inc., 1987. http://www.lds.org/music/library/childrens-songbook/ill-walk-with-you?lang=eng

Sensory Processing Disorder Foundation. "About SPD." Accessed January 5, 2014. http://www.spdfoundation.net/about-sensory-processing-disorder.html

Parting Thoughts ✍

When I was growing up with Crystal, I didn't have anyone who could relate to my situation. My mom had counsel for me all along the way, and she was very patient with my questions and frustrations. My other siblings would play and fight with me, so I knew what the "normal" home and family experience was like. I also had friends and enemies at school just like anyone else.

What I didn't have was someone to whom I felt I could relate, someone who knew what I was going through. People were sympathetic, but that's not the same as being empathetic. Maybe for you, this book can be that companion I never had. It's hard to have a conversation with a book, but we can hopefully work through this together.

If nothing else, remember that it isn't your fault that your sibling does what he or she does and that you're not the only one who's ever felt the way you do. Also remember that your reactions to these situations do matter and that it can get better with time. As long as you're doing your best, you're doing great!

I hope that you will connect with me and my other siblings online on Facebook, Twitter, GoodReads, and at http://www.ashley-nance.com. I look forward to seeing you there!

Appendix 2

A Chat with Crystal ∽

I have interviewed Crystal about her experiences in school to include as part of a presentation that I was preparing to give at school. I include it here because it is instructive and so that you can get to know Crystal by "hearing" about things from her perspective. The following interview was conducted through instant messenger, so it has been left in its original, unedited form.

Ashley: hi there

Crystal: Hi Ashley

Ashley: how are you?

Crystal: I am fine

Ashley: hi Crystal
you haven't gone to bed yet?

Crystal: Hi Anything in particular you want to talk about?

Ashley: yeah I was curious about some stuff about when you were ins school

Crystal: Really? like what?
No I havent gone to bed yet

Ashley: should you? I know it's late and I can do this now or Monday
It'll only take a couple minutes though

Crystal: I'm fine. you can do it now

Ashley: ok cool
When you were in Elementary school did you take any special education classes?

Crystal: Yes I even remember the teachers names if you want em

Ashley: sure

Crystal: In Dix avenue it was miss? Goldy and Mrs? Gould. In Horizon Heights it was Mrs? Barcena. As you can see, i didnt really pay attention to their marital status

Ashley: That's ok :)
At Dix Avenue did you go to resource room or did they come into the class-room?

Crystal: I went to them

Ashley: what did you do there?

Crystal: Not alot mostly learned stuff at a slower pace but it usually wasnt anything reallyimportant
At least thats what i remember

Ashley: ok
in the classroom with everybody else did you feel like you were included with their activities and learning?

Crystal: sometimes yes and sometimes no there were cetain things that only some people needed to learn but there were some things that every body did

Ashley: what do you mean?

Crystal: Like there were somme people that neede to learn how to read,but not all of us so there would be groups of people doing different things Im sorry ive been desribing what happened at Horizon Heights

Ashley: ok
so you already knew how to read so you didn't have to be in a reading group. Like that?

Crystal: exactly did you read what I wrote at the end of my previous statement?

Ashley: yes
so what about at Dix Avenue?
Did you feel included in activities and learning there?

Crystal: I dont have alot of memories about that because it wasnt exciting at all I just remember getting prizes for doing something well
yes but it wasnt hard because ther were only 3 or 4 people in there

Ashley: in the resource room or in the general classroom?

Crystal: In resource room

Ashley: in Dix Avenue, about how much of the day did you spend in resource room?

Crystal: not alot probably an hour or so

Ashley: ok
what about the rest of the day? Did you feel included in the general classroom with the other students that didn't go to resource?

Crystal: yes

Ashley: in what ways were you included?

Crystal: I dont know all I know is that I didnt feel left out at all

Ashley: that's good
same at Horizon Heights?

Crystal: Not really because sometimes they would do fun activities when I was in mrs Barcenas

Ashley: like what?

Crystal: I dont really remember anyting in particular

Ashley: that's fine
do you think you needed that time in the resource room to help you?

Crystal: not really because most of the time we werent learning anything in there that we would learn in the classroom

Ashley: so you'd go to resource to learn stuff they were learning in the regular clasroom?

Crystal: what
?

Ashley: I was clarifying. Is that what you meant?

Crystal: no it was the opposite of what you said

Ashley: so you think you did need the time in resource room?

Crystal: no not really

Ashley: I gues it's the why not that confuses me

Crystal: what?

Ashley: could you tell me again - why you feel like you didn't need to go to resource room?

Crystal: because i wasnt learning anything important

Ashley: ok
changing subjects a little
how about middle school?

Crystal: midle school wqas a whole diferent story

Ashley: tell me about it

Crystal: Wel part of the reson why it was so different was because of Miss Romero. She was very strict and she was teaching us high level stuff. Do you want to know about Mrs.Peck too
?

Ashley: first middle school
I don't know anything about your middle school experience
how much time did you spend with Ms. Romero each day?

Crystal: She was my teacher for more of middle school than Miss Romero was

Ashley: oh yeah huh

Crystal: Only one period

Ashley: ok
did you learn important stuff in there?

Crystal: not really, You mean in Miss Romeros?

Ashley: yes

Crystal: The only thing I remember learning about was the different shapes like a hexagon and a rhombus

Ashley: ok
Do you feel like you needed the time in there to help you learn?

Crystal: Not really

Ashley: why not?

Crystal: Because like before I wasnt learning anything that I needed to know.

Ashley: ok
how about with Mrs. Peck?

Crystal: Well with Mrs Peck I started going there more often like spendin more time every day withh her

Ashley: was that helpful?

Crystal: yes

Ashley: why is that?

Crystal: because she was teaching me things I did need to know

Ashley: what was the difference do you think?

Crystal: I guess she had more of an idea of what I needed personally

Ashley: I see
what about in your other classes? In Clarke and Hartford did you feel like you were included in your other classes?

Crystal: Not really because even with all the stuff I was learning,I was still behind

Ashley: did you feel like an important part of the class? Did the teachers and other students involve you?

Crystal: No because they hated me

Ashley: the students or the teachers?

Crystal: Not the teachers but the students

Ashley: why did they hate you?

Crystal: I have no idea some hated me from the first day.I never did figure it out

Ashley: sad

Crystal: Yes very

Ashley: awsome. Well, if it's ok with you, I want to share what I learned from you today with other students who are studying to become educators

Crystal: Thats fine glad I could help my sister that I love so much!

Ashley: yay!
Is there any other things you would like these students to know?

Crystal: Yay

Ashley: Is there any other things you would like these students to know?

Crystal: I have to think

Ashley: If you could tell someone who was going to be a teacher some day anything you wanted, what would you tell them?

Crystal: Do not judge them They need love just like anyone else
I hope they can be like Mrs O Conner in every way

Except her yelling at Lindsey and Corrine

Ashley: IN what ways?

Crystal: Her loving gentle ways. She was like a second mother to me you know

Ashley: really?

Crystal: Yes
I thought you still remembered that about her

Ashley: i do
but i want to hear it from you :)

Crystal: Thats good I was starting to worry for a moment there

Ashley: :)

That's ok

anything else you want to tell them?

Crystal: No

Ashley: ok
thank you very much you helped me understand some things about students being included in their schools
I love you!

Crystal: Love you to Asholee you are very welcom

Ashley: It's late I'm sorry. I'll let you go to bed.

Crystal: Thank ya much

Ashley: no fair reading anything but the scriptures, morning comes early. alright?

Crystal: oooookayyyyyy

Ashley: :D
we should chat again some time this is fun

Crystal: yeah it is

Ashley: ok
goodnight Crystal
sweet dreams!

Crystal: Night Asley same to you
Sorry I spelled yourbname wrong

Ashley: that's ok
bye

About Familius

Welcome to a place where mothers are celebrated, not compared. Where heart is at the center of our families, and family at the center of our homes. Where boo boos are still kissed, cake beaters are still licked, and mistakes are still okay. Welcome to a place where books—and family—are beautiful. Familius: a book publisher dedicated to helping families be happy.

Visit Our Website: www.familius.com

Our website is a different kind of place. Get inspired, read articles, discover books, watch videos, connect with our family experts, download books and apps and audiobooks, and along the way, discover how values and happy family life go together.

Join Our Family

There are lots of ways to connect with us! Subscribe to our newsletters at www.familius.com to receive uplifting daily inspiration, essays from our Pater Familius, a free ebook every month, and the first word on special discounts and Familius news.

Become an Expert

Familius authors and other established writers interested in helping families be happy are invited to join our family and contribute online content. If you have something important to say on the family, join our expert community by applying at:

www.familius.com/apply-to-become-a-familius-expert

Get Bulk Discounts

If you feel a few friends and family might benefit from what you've read, let us know and we'll be happy to provide you with quantity discounts. Simply email us at specialorders@familius.com.

Website: www.familius.com

Facebook: www.facebook.com/paterfamilius

Twitter: @familiustalk, @paterfamilius1

Pinterest: www.pinterest.com/familius

The most important work

you ever do will be within the

walls of your own home.

CPSIA information can be obtained at www.ICGtesting.com
Printed in the USA
BVOW07s1902160614

356377BV00004B/38/P